Creating Stories for Storytelling

Marsh Cassady

Resource Publications, Inc.
San Jose, California

Editorial director: Kenneth Guentert
Managing editor: Kathi Drolet
Production: Elizabeth J. Asborno

Reprint Department
Resource Publications, Inc.
160 E. Virginia Street, #290
San Jose, CA 95112-5848

Library of Congress Cataloging in Publication Data
    Cassady, Marsh, 1936-
    Creating stories for storytelling / Marsh Cassady.
        p.   cm.
    Includes bibliographical references.
    ISBN 0-89390-205-5
    1. Creative writing.   2. Storytelling.   I. Title
  PN145.C335   1991
808.5'43—dc20   91-3627
                                                              CIP

5 4 3 2 1 | 95 94 93 92 91

To Kate, Shannon, and Gary
May all your stories have happy endings

Contents

Acknowledgments

The stories or story excerpts in this book are reprinted with permission from their copyright holders:

"Messages" by Richard L. Stone, *Crazyquilt* (December 1988), reprinted with permission from the author; "Maps" by Michael Langley, *Crazyquilt* (March 1989), reprinted with permission from the author; "A Beautiful Man" by Cathryn Alpert, *Crazyquilt* (September 1989), reprinted with permission from the author; "Going Fishing" by Marsh Cassady, *Green's Magazine* (September 1987), reprinted with permission from the publisher; "Love So Amazing, So Divine" by Amy Belding Brown, *Crazyquilt* (September 1988), reprinted with permission from the author; "Pathosphere" by David F. Hamilton and Peter W. Telep, *Crazyquilt* (June 1989), reprinted with permission from the author; "Giantess" by Mimi Albert, *Crazyquilt* (September 1988), reprinted with permission from the author; "The Pleiades" by Jerine Watson-Miner, *Crazyquilt* (September 1988), reprinted with permission from the author; "Song of the Dog" by March Cassady, *Ciccada* (Fall 1986), reprinted with permission from the publisher; "The Mad Countess" by Mary Louise R. O'Hara, *Crazyquilt* (December 1987), reprinted with permission from the author; "Lucretia Matilda Penelope Snort and Her Booglie Wooglie Wagon" by Jean R. Seley, reprinted with permission from the author; "Ol' Sam's

Secret" by James Henderschedt, *The Magic Stone and Other Stories for Your Faith Journey* (Resource Publications, Inc., 1988), reprinted with permission from the publisher; "The Cup" by Joseph J. Juknialis, *A Stillness Without Shadows* (Resource Publications, Inc., 1986), reprinted with permission from the publisher; "Balloons! Candy! Toys!" by Daryl Olszewski, *Balloons! Candy! Toys!* (Resource Publications, Inc., 1986), reprinted with permission from the publisher; *Once Upon an Eternity*, chapters 7 and 9, by David Edman (Resource Publications, Inc., 1984), reprinted with permission from the publisher; "Carved out of Love and Shaped into Stories" by Joseph J. Juknialis, *When God Began in the Middle* (Resource Publications, Inc., 1982), reprinted with permission from the publisher; "An Iffy Situation" by Marsh Cassady, *Buckeye Country* (Summer 1978), reprinted with permission from the author; "Johnny and the Monster" by Marsh Cassady, *Candle* (May 1986), reprinted with permission from the author; "Curve of a Dreamer" by Jacqueline Cicchetti and Bill Jarosin, *Poems* (Hana Press, 1986), reprinted with permission from the authors; "Tonight My Sister Danced Freedom" by Marsh Cassady (KPBS Radio, San Diego, July 8, 1988), reprinted with permission from the author; "Whose Woods These Are" by Marsh Cassady, *Buffalo Spree* (Fall 1987), reprinted with permission from the author.

Preface

I have spent many years of my life with stories—reading them, listening to them, telling them, writing them.

Before moving to California in 1980, I spent the preceding three years telling stories to any groups or organizations who would agree to listen. I must have averaged a telling a week—to women's groups, senior citizens, business organizations. I spun my tales in restaurants, convention centers, and halls. Some of the stories were my own; others I'd read or heard.

Stories are important to me. So I've tried to make them important to others, as well, through teaching college courses both on how to tell them and how to write them, and through my own writing and telling.

If you create a story, after all, you create the world—or many worlds.

One

Audience and Purpose

"Once upon a time..."

"Many years ago in a far off kingdom..."

"Did you hear the one about..."

"A funny thing happened to me..."

"It was the best of times; it was the worst of times..."

"Once upon a midnight dreary, as I pondered..."

"'Twas the night before Christmas and all through the house..."

"And He said, 'A certain man had two sons...'"

Stories illustrate truths, provide examples to live by, entertain, teach us the meaning of life.

They are told at religious services, at schools, at meetings, around campfires. Anywhere people gather, stories are told.

What do all the stories we hear have in common? Some are as little as two lines; some have complicated plots and take a long time to tell. Some are largely to entertain, others to teach or reinforce values.

Yet the one thing they all have in common is that they contain universals truths, aspects of life with which we can identify. In other words, they have meaning for us; there is a point to them.

Determining Purpose

Two quite different stories follow. Yet each can and has been presented by storytellers. The first one occurs in Japan.

SONG OF THE DOG

by Marsh Cassady

Kazu sang a song of her own making after being informed of Eiji's death. Where she left off, the pair of parakeets her dead husband had given her took up the melody. She opened the door of their cage and placed the birds in her hands, feeling the beat of their hearts as a counterpoint to her own pulse. The birds refused to fly away when she slid open the panel of the door to her home. It was important, she knew, that they soar away to be with Eiji. She gave them a gentle nudge. Reproachfully, they gazed at her. They finally hopped to the sill, then took flight. As they lost themselves in the dark of the night, she wept.

Friends brought Kazu fruit or other round objects symbolizing life's cycle. She greeted them with a fixed smile for no Japanese woman of breeding can inflict her grief upon others.

Yet Kazu could still feel Eiji's spirit nearby, hungering for her as she hungered for him.

Two terns were afloat in the sky. Their wings caught the light streaming from behind the horizon. The distant mountain stood out in clear relief, bathing the water in mellow golden light.

The tide rose and fell throughout Naruto's narrow channel, forming the western entrance to the Inland Sea from the Pacific, its strange, compelling beauty reaching toward her. Masses of green and white dwarfed pine sought the sky.

Kazu walked until stars appeared.

A dog, lean and hungry, followed Kazu home. He licked her hand and then the tears from her face. He refused to leave and slept all night on the sill outside the door.

Foggy masses of clouds filled the early morning sky. A drizzle coated the landscape like mother-of-pearl.

As the dog walked with her to the temple grounds, the sun burned off the fog.

Along the deserted shores of the Inland Sea the dog sniffed, running ahead, stopping to see if she followed. She tossed a stick to him. He brought it back. She tossed it once more.

She threw the stick too close to the water, and the tide swept it out. "Come back!" she shouted as the dog dashed into the sea. "Come back, foolish dog."

He was caught in a bed of kelp. She saw him struggling to free himself. A wave cut off his yelp, breaking directly on top of him. She jumped in after him. A wave swelled under her, lifting her, pushing her forward. The water from the previous waves had receded into the foot of her wave, leaving it twice as tall as the others. She could not possibly turn back now without getting torn apart by the hard blue wall.

The dog appeared drowned, momentarily hanging like something dead inside the circle of her arm. Belatedly, his body became alive against her, and he became entangled in the sleeve of her kimono. Gasping and flailing, she herself became caught in the huge bed of kelp.

Spinning and churning, the wave smashed her into the hard wet sand of the seabed. She had no energy left to struggle.

On the outer layer of the water she saw the sunlight sparkling like tiny golden stars. She recognized in them the sign of God, a sign of love, a sign of truth. And immediately she was at peace. The water was ice-blue silk.

"Thank you, Lord Buddha," she whispered, "for the excuse."

JOHNNY AND THE MONSTER

by Marsh Cassady

Johnny was walking along the sidewalk when suddenly the monster jumped right out and blocked his path.

"Boo," it yelled and waved its arms.

"Oh, hi," Johnny said, trying to step around it.

"Aren't you afraid of me?" the creature asked.

"Should I be?"

"Everybody is."

"Everybody?"

"Well, sort of." The creature smiled, its teeth like giant grains of corn, square in the middle of its big green face. "I try to scare people, but I'm not really successful."

"I can understand that," Johnny said. "I'm not successful either."

The creature held out his hand. "My name is Xyssth. You can call me Bob."

"I'm Johnny." He and Bob shook hands. "So where are you from?" Johnny asked.

"The other side of the moon."

"Oh, come on. There's no air there. You couldn't breathe."

"Not your moon. Another one far, far away."

"Sure."

"It's true," the monster said.

"Why did you try to frighten me?"

"I want to live on Xyllt."

"What's that?" Johnny asked.

"A planet. Like earth. But everyone is so scary there that—I don't think you'd understand."

"Yes, I would."

"You have to be scary to live there. So everyone has to take a test for scaring people. And if you don't succeed, you live on the moon forever. It's

lonely, away from moms and dads and cousins. It's
ever so much better on Xyllt."

"It seems like you have a problem," Johnny said.
"But then doesn't everyone?"

"Do you?"

Johnny sighed. "I sure do. Back in New Jersey I
had friends. Lots of them. But nobody likes me
here. They say I talk funny. I have an accent."

"Maybe they just have to learn to know you."

"You think it's easy to make friends?"

"We're talking, aren't we?" The creature snorted.
"Everyone becomes my friend, and I can't scare
anyone."

Just then a space ship landed, right beside Johnny
and Bob. A beam shot out and teleported Johnny
inside. As soon as he showed up, the creatures
there, all of whom looked like Bob, suddenly began
to scream. They covered their faces with their
hands and tried to hide in the corners. Johnny had
never seen anyone look so frightened.

He tried to talk to them, and finally they calmed
down. "It's okay," he said. "I don't want to hurt
you. I think you meant to get Bob?"

"Who?" one of the green men croaked.

"Your friend, Bob."

"Oh, yes, you mean Xyssth. Everybody's friend."

"Let me out of here," Johnny said, "and I'll bring
him back for you."

One of the creatures pushed a button and the
door opened. Johnny ran outside and up to Bob.

"They wanted you, but got me." Johnny grabbed
Bob's arm and led him up the ramp. Just then two
girls Johnny recognized came by. They were in his
homeroom at school. They watched Johnny drag
Bob up the ramp. Then they began to scream, and
Johnny saw them run away.

"Well, Xyssth," the commander of the ship said, "I
suppose you passed the test since there's nothing

in the rules about how you scare people. Even if it means having someone else do it for you."

"I don't know what you—" Johnny stomped on Bob's foot to make him hush.

"Of course, we should have known that your friend here never meant to harm us," the commander said. "So I suppose you've passed and can live on Xyllt." He turned to the control panel. "Say goodbye to your friend. We have to be heading home."

"See, Bob," Johnny said, "it all worked out."

"I don't know how I can ever thank you."

"That's what friends are for. To help each other. At least your problem's solved."

"If you want me to, I'll stay and try to help you."

"Oh, no, Bob," Johnny answered. "I know you'd like to get home."

Johnny turned and walked down the ramp. As soon as he was away from the ship, it soared into the sky. It became a tiny speck and then disappeared.

Johnny turned and started to school, head down, hands in his pocket. Then he heard someone call. Up ahead he saw a group of his classmates.

"Is it true, Johnny?" one of them asked.

"Is what true?" Johnny was puzzled.

"That there was an alien invasion. And you dragged the invader back to his ship. All by yourself."

"Oh, no, it wasn't—"

Brenda, one of the girls who'd passed by the ship, interrupted. "You should have seen him," she said. "He was so brave."

In the cafeteria at lunchtime there were several big arguments before it was decided who would sit next to Johnny.

As you see, the two stories are not at all similar; they have different purposes and so would appeal to different audiences.

The most important consideration when planning to tell a story is to consider the audience and the purpose. Often, they are closely related. If, for example, you want to tell a story in a religious education class, you have a set audience, a group of young people, and a purpose, a learning experience.

Of course, you will want to be more specific than that. What is it exactly that you want to point out to the class? Once you decide, you either devise a story of your own or look for one that fits the purpose.

Similarly, if you want to illustrate a point in a speech you are making to a service organization, you make sure you have an appropriate story.

Fitting the Story to the Occasion

Appropriateness is an important consideration. The first of the two stories in this chapter would not be appropriate for a group of small children. Yet you may want to bring home the same point to them.

What is the point of this story? It has to do both with loneliness and the grieving process. It is universal in that no matter when or where a person lives, he or she feels similarly. Certainly, this is something to be considered by people of all ages. Yet preschoolers or kids below the age of twelve or so probably would find the story boring. There are parts of it they would fail to understand. Not so for adults.

Then how could this story be used? I used it once in a reading I gave to a group of senior citizens. The idea there was that all of us at times are lonely, and all of us grieve. This means we are not alone. The realization that this is true may help dispel our feelings of isolation.

I used the same story when I taught a continuing education class in creative writing. I wanted the students to be able to identify with a woman from an alien culture. Through far removed in both space and time, still she felt the same sort of things students in the class may have felt or could feel.

The point is that how you introduce the story and what you say at the end bear directly on your purpose. The same story can be made to fit any number of occasions, depending on the circumstances and reasons for meeting.

Most stories entertain us, and that may be the only purpose. Or at least the primary purpose. Yet, they also contain universal truths. Certainly, you could tell either of the two stories simply for entertainment, to immerse the listener into situations he or she will never actually encounter. But most often, if there is no meat to what you present, the listener is going to leave feeling cheated or empty.

Why Stories Are Told

If you listen to any public speech, no matter what the occasion, from a religious service to a political rally, more than likely you will hear the speaker tell at least one story, whether a joke or a tale with a well-defined plot and characters.

Why do you suppose this is so? Why not simply state the facts or the message?

First, stories stick in our memories. They are a painless way of learning and are much more interesting than unembellished statements of fact or opinion.

And, of course, there are many situations in which the story is its own purpose. There is a resurgence lately of the art of storytelling simply for pleasure and entertainment. There are storytellers who travel from community to community, speaking at churches and schools. Most libraries now have story hours for children, in which a person, whether or not a library employee, reads or tells stories.

You have to decide on your reasons. What group is your story for? Why do you want to tell the members a story? What sort of response do you hope to elicit from the group? What changes do you want to bring about by telling the story?

Every experience we have alters us, whether minutely or greatly. In what way do you want to alter the people to whom you tell a story? Do you want to teach them about life? Do you want to change their thinking on a certain issue? Do you want them to change their behavior in some way? Of course, there is no way to list all the possible types of change a person may wish to bring about. But in each situation, to be effective the storyteller needs to plan out what it is he or she wants to do and how best to reach this goal.

"Johnny and the Monster" has several "morals." One is that it is important to our well being to make friends. Another is that there are often far-reaching effects of our kindnesses. Johnny for a moment put the concerns of Bob above his own concerns, and in so doing, brought about a change in how others thought of him. Do unto others, and often it will be done unto you.

The first step in becoming an effective storyteller is to understand and analyze your reasons for telling the story. Once you've done that, the rest more easily falls into place.

Two

Discovering and Developing Ideas

You have analyzed the situation and the audience and decided on your purpose in telling a story. What do you do next?

Getting Ideas

I was walking down the street in San Diego the other day, glancing out across the sunlit Pacific, watching kids and dogs romping on the beach, thinking about a story I want to develop for a talk I'm going to give. Suddenly, a little man in a shabby suit coat and torn jeans came up and stood squarely in my path.

"Excuse me," I said, trying to step around him, knowing it was he who should yield. But I was in a mellow mood and not up to sparring with little leprechaun types.

He blocked my path again. "Have I got a deal for you!" he said in a high squeaky voice. I expected him to open his coat and show me a row of cheap watches or fake-diamond necklaces. But no such thing.

> For the first time, I saw that he carried long glass tubes, maybe a dozen of them, in his left hand. I guess I hadn't noticed previously because they were transparent.
>
> He saw the direction of my gaze and chuckled. "They're ideas," he said. "Elusive, hard to pin down. But captured here forever in glass...or at least till you want to take them out and use them." He peered closely up into my eyes. "How about it?" he asked. "They might do wonders for you. Only a dime a dozen!"

Ideas are a dime a dozen. They come from something in our present or past and are triggered by what we see, read, or experience. If you are a person who likes to tell stories or is in an occupation where storytelling is used, you need to gear yourself to look for ideas.

We receive them constantly. The trouble is we are so used to blocking them out as soon as they touch our conscious thinking, that we often don't even recognize them. Certainly, not all the ideas that come to us are worth developing. But if we get into the habit of squelching them right away, we may be setting a pattern in which we begin to ignore all ideas, almost subliminally.

Once you gear yourself to look for ideas, they literally can come from any experience. Once I saw an old woman walking along a back street, carrying an armful of long-stemmed roses, reminiscent of Miss America Pageants. From this came a story I called "A Walk in Beauty." It's a tale of a future society in which old age is the standard of beauty.

What was the point of this story? I presented it to several groups, reinforcing what we all know but sometimes ignore. Old people *are* beautiful, maybe not so much by generally accepted standards of beauty, but within. The story is a kind of satirical piece, in which the beauty queen finally realizes that she does not possess physical beauty, but rather a more enduring kind.

Make up your mind to recognize ideas when they come to you. Write them down to make yourself constantly aware of them. All of us can condition ourselves to get ideas that excite us. Of course, we will conceive others as well, those that either are unimportant or don't hold our interest. Certainly, we will discard more ideas than we will use. But if we discard all of them first, we have nothing to develop.

Recognizing ideas involves an openness to all sensory stimuli. You need to cultivate a sensitivity to others, to your surroundings, and to yourself. What bothers you about what you perceive? What excites you? How can you take these things and develop them into stories?

Besides gearing yourself to look for ideas, there are many techniques you can use to stimulate your imagination.

Examining the Past

You often can use what you observe in the present to call up the past. This is what poet Jacqueline Cicchetti did after seeing an old building in Los Angeles. Here is the last section of her poem, "The Curve of a Dreamer."

> How streaked with years, the bricks.
> But those stairs
> the way they curve at the bottom
> turned by some dreamer
> for people who lived there so long ago.
> Almost I see their faces
> and for a moment I walk and laugh

with men and women a hundred years gone.
Alone in my car on this busy downtown street
I stare at an empty building
hemmed in by factories
and around me drifts the odor
of ancient lilacs.

Another person seeing the building just as easily could invent a background for the imagined people who live there and develop a story involving these people.

Cicchetti's poem evokes the past in general. But often something reminds us of our own pasts. We hear a snatch of an old song that brings back memories. Or a look on someone's face reminds us of a long-ago friend.

Once I saw a toy monkey that reminded me of a stuffed animal I owned years ago. My aunt worked for Goodwill Industries in Pittsburgh. One of the other people there was a man called Richard. His job was to restore old toys for resale in the Goodwill Store.

When I met him, I was about eight years old. Richard's legs were twisted and deformed, and he scooted from place to place in a little cart on castors. He invited me into his workroom to see all the toys and told me I could choose one to keep. I chose a monkey that was missing one eye.

Later, back home in the town where I grew up, I had the monkey with me on the front porch. A friend came by, and I was ashamed to have him see I still played with stuffed animals. I pretended the monkey was some sort of ball to toss up in the air. We threw it back and forth, and each time we missed and it slammed into the ground, I felt as if a little of myself was somehow being torn away. It wasn't that the monkey itself meant so much to me. It was that it came from a man I'd liked.

All these memories were triggered by seeing a stuffed animal in a store window. Now how could I develop this into a story? Well, it might be something about being true to self and to people we like. It might be about guilt, about peer pressure, or it might simply be a nostalgic remembrance.

This happened spontaneously, but you can consciously evoke the past. A friend asked me once why I didn't use my own childhood as the basis of my stories. Why indeed? The result of his question was that I consciously tried to remember whatever I could from various ages of my life.

One of the resulting stories is "Whose Woods These Are."[1] I've told the story to various groups, and it has been twice published. I started out with a simple goal, to develop an idea from one of the places I loved as a child, my grandfather's farm.

Although the events of the story are based in reality, I am not at all like the central character. The reason for creating such a story? One is to show that a rather minor occurrence in the past can continue to affect us through the years.

What occurred was that the father of a young boy is thrown into a muddy bank by his cousin, using jujitsu. The boy witnesses what happens and begins to hate the cousin for destroying the boy's idolization of his father. At the same time he hates his father for being no more than a mere human being.

---

1. I refer to this story throughout the book. Therefore, I have put it in the Appendix so you can read it in its entirety and better grasp its meaning and nuances.

The boy, now a middle-aged man, has let this occurrence affect the rest of his life, making few friends, but determined not to show any weakness.

In this story I remembered something in my own past, my grandfather's farm, and the fact that my father was interested in jujitsu. Most of the rest is pure invention.

Ideas are pretty easy to come by, but, as I implied at the beginning of the chapter, in themselves they are worth little. It's what you do with them that matters. For instance, when I began "Johnny and the Monster," I knew only that I wanted to express the importance of friendship and of "loving one another."

I knew also that I wanted to end up with a story I could tell to kids. What would interest them? Maybe a story about a boy who moved far away from home and is lonely. This was a logical premise because in today's mobile society, people rarely remain in one dwelling more than a few years.

Okay, I had a character and the beginnings of a situation. To intensify Johnny's feelings, I had him move to a non-specified place where even the manner of speaking was different.

Kids like stories with upbeat endings. So, of course, I wanted the story to end with everyone happy.

Obviously, this couldn't happen spontaneously, or there'd be no story. What could I do?

I've always liked science fiction, and I've found that most children I know like monsters or alien beings. All right, I'd have a sort of klutzy character from outer space, who seemingly had just the opposite kind of problem. He made friends too easily.

The two characters come together and what happens? They become fast friends. The alien discovers that even though he has tried not to make friends, friendship is really pretty important. And as a direct result of the boy's friendship with him, both resolve their problems.

Many of the ideas I've used both in my storytelling and in my writing have come from the past, from events, places, and people that were simply there.

Generally, I've used this sort of thing in developing stories for adults, basing my children's stories more on specific themes. On the other hand, Jean Seley developed a children's story through remembering bits of her past and then using exaggeration to build a specific character.

When Jean was a teenager, she lived in a mountain area that had many summer tourists. There was an eccentric old woman who lived there as well.

LUCRETIA MATILDA PENELOPE SNORT AND HER BOOGLIE WOOGLIE WAGON

by Jean Seley

Lucretia Matilda Penelope Snort sniffed the evening air. Cherry Cola, yes, it was definitely Cherry Cola.

"Aha!" she shouted to the pine trees. "The Summer Wimmets!" The pine trees shuddered with the sound of distant applause as a gust of chilly evening air tumbled past Miss Snort, stirred by the mention of Summer Wimmets.

"Coming soon, yes, coming soon. Be calm," she soothed. "Be calm," she whispered. And the gust of chilly air settled in the grass near the road. The pine trees sighed, then were still.

Lucretia Matilda Penelope Snort turned left and marched up the bumpy road home pulling her Booglie Wooglie Wagon. It was made from scraps of wood and baby buggy wheels and loaded with rags, brushes, pails and cleaning potions. Every day Miss Snort left her home at first glimpse of dawn to clean the mountain cabins of people living in these woods called Twain Harte.

"Time's passing. We must be home. Must be home," Lucretia Matilda said. The Booglie Wooglie wagon answered with a clink, a clang and a clatter.

The ground squirrels and wood rats skittered to hide behind pine trees as Lucretia Matilda Penelope Snort and her Booglie Wooglie wagon rattled and clattered up the road, shattering the quiet of early evening.

Her black skirt swirled around her high top boots, and the red silk rose that was perched on the center of her black fur hat, bobbed up and down as she walked.

Lucretia Snort has a whole series of adventures, all brought to mind by the author's memories.

Often you can go back to much earlier years for experiences that were of particular importance to you. Then ask yourself: How has this affected me? How do I feel about it? In what way am I like others in how I feel and in what happened to me? Does what I say really have importance for others? If you think it does have meaning, go ahead and develop it.

Be Aware of the World Around You

Another way to get ideas is to make yourself more aware of the world around you. You need to look at the world through new eyes, to see the unexpected, the different, the new. Doing this not only helps interpret life more clearly, but it makes it more interesting as well.

You need to look at the world with a fresh perspective. As Dorthea Brande suggests in her book *On Becoming a Writer*: "It will be worth your while to walk on strange streets, to visit exhibits, to hunt up a movie in a strange part of town in order to give yourself the experience of fresh seeing once or twice a week."

Another way of developing a fresh perspective is through roleplaying, not only to examine attitudes, but to try to actually see the world as others do. Try to look at everyday events and surroundings through someone else's eyes. Walk or drive down the street, looking at houses and stores as a foreigner, as your grandfather, as a friend, as someone who's never seen apartment buildings or huge shopping malls. What seems different to you now? In what way?

Take what you have seen as someone else and analyze your thoughts and feelings. Then use them as the basis of a story.

It can help to keep a journal, including thoughts and events but going further. Keep a record of people and behaviors. Periodically, check back over what you've written. An acquaintance keeps a three-ring binder stuffed with short character sketches of people he observes. He writes down traits as well as actions. Just by this mere fact he learns much about human nature. Whether or not he ever uses any of these people as the basis of a story, he has taught himself to be aware of what people are like in a variety of situations. He analyzes and later can draw upon what he has learned, often without conscious effort.

Actually, anything you do that makes you more aware is bound to be helpful in getting ideas for stories. The following exercises can help you find and develop ideas.

1. Carry a notepad with you. For the next week, try to come up with at least two ideas a day, ideas that could provide the basis for a story. Don't be judgmental. When an idea comes to you, jot it down. Don't try to decide if it's good or not or even whether you want to work with it. Instead, this exercise should be a free association kind of thing with the purpose of teaching you to be aware.

During the second week, jot down three or four ideas a day; during the third week, five or six. This may sound difficult, but it isn't. The problem is that everyone gets into the pattern of squelching ideas almost before they become conscious thought.

A friend of mine invented a plunger to be used with windshield washers on cars. For several years he received four dollars on nearly every American brand automobile sold. He told me that he does not think of his ideas as unique. He simply has the facilities to develop them.

If you concentrate on spotting ideas, you'll find it becomes easier and easier. Only then should you begin to judge them. If any of them particularly appeal to you, go ahead and develop them.

2. Get into the habit of looking through newspapers each day for ideas. I have a writer/actor/director friend who relies almost entirely on newspapers for his ideas. He once read a short item in the *Los Angeles Times* about someone stealing a house. He started asking himself questions about this and came up with the idea for a screen play. He asked such things as: What type of person would steal a house? Why? Where would a person take it? What would he or she do with it?

3. It's been said that in order to be creative in finding ideas, you should learn to look at your surroundings as if seeing them for the first time. I suggest the opposite. Look at people and objects as if you are seeing them for the last time. Since you'll never see them again, you'll want to memorize and remember all the details. Once you try this, write an interpretive description of what you've observed: as a straightforward observation; as a character other than yourself; as part of a story in which someone else is making the observations.

4. Tear down a stereotype. Find someone who doesn't fit the pattern you've been led by society or your environment to believe exists. How does the particular person not fit the stereotype? Write a character sketch in which you show how he or she

is different. Then develop a story idea in which the difference is apparent.

5. Evoke the past in general. Look at an old building, a book at an antiquarian book store, or an exhibit at a museum. Pretend the object you observe is new rather than old. What do you feel? What other people do you see in this "scene?" What are they doing? What is the environment in general like? Develop a story about one of the characters you imagined there.

6. Evoke your own past. Get into the habit of spending five minutes each day searching your own memory and thinking about a specific time. Or look at an object that relates to your past: a photograph, a piece of clothing, a book you've kept. Remember the circumstances of each. Who took the photograph? Who is in it? Why was it taken? What did it mean to you then? What does it mean to you now? Why? Take one of the things you've recalled and use it as a starting point for a story.

Develop a nostalgia piece from what you discover.

7. Look at a landscape painting or photograph until you imagine yourself drawn into the scene. Then experience your surroundings as completely as you can. Touch and see and hear and smell and talk with. "Interview" any persons in the painting or photo about their lives, asking questions about any aspects that interest you. Build a biography of these people. Then more carefully examine the surroundings. What are your feelings about them, or about each specific object in them? Do they give you a feeling of serenity, or perhaps one of terror? Now

develop a story idea based on what you've "experienced" in the location.

Often in creating a scene of the imagination, you will begin with what is observable, as if watching a play being enacted, but then simply let the play take over and run its course.

8. Begin to keep a dream journal. Get up fifteen minutes early one or two days a week and write down what you remember from your dreams. With practice you can remember more and more material, which often works as the basis for stories.

9. Play the "what if" game with yourself. What if I had a million dollars? What if I suddenly found a secret map? What if I were a basketball star and could make all my shots up to a certain point, but later could make no shots at all?

This last question is one I used in developing a story called "An Iffy Situation." The main character is a young woman who likes to play "what if." The opening scene follows:

> Gladys Hinkle couldn't help it. Every time she was by herself she played the "what if" game. The rules were simple. Take any situation and change it around. The sun always set in the west and rose in the east. Water ran downhill. People grew older. But what if?
>
> What if she were a member of the Boston Celtics? What if she hit her first thirty shots each day but always missed after that?
>
> What if people grew younger instead of older? It would make for an interesting world.
>
> That was the trouble. The world just wasn't an interesting place.

Now what if you had written that opening to a story? Where would you go with it? There are many possibilities. What if some of the "what ifs" came true? What if Gladys met someone else who played the "what if" game?

In my story, Gladys actually found that things really weren't so bad and the world was interesting, after all. So the story was about learning to live with the conditions of life that can't be changed.

Further Ideas

Many ideas come from relaxing and daydreaming. The Bible says: "Your old men see visions, and your young men dream dreams." And why not, despite always being cautioned as children not to daydream but to be "practical."

Many times, abandoning oneself to a daydream or fantasy has been called an altered state of consciousness, just as nightdreaming is. There have been societies where people believed that such visions were another form of reality.

When daydreaming or creating fantasies, it helps to break the rules. Make fish meow or water run uphill. According to Robert McKim in *Experiences in Visual Thinking,* "By defying reality, this distinction between reality and imagination is clarified and your ability to control imagination is strengthened."

So far you've been given many ideas for getting ideas. But then what? In developing them into a finished form, a lot depends on your interests. I like science fiction and fantasy and so tend to think of or gear ideas to that genre of storytelling. I consciously decide that I want ideas to fit a particular framework and that's the kind of ideas that begin to occur to me. In other words, I develop a particular "mind set." It seems almost magical, but it's as if my whole being is now in a particular mode or gear, and much of the work is done without conscious thought.

Often, ideas need time to incubate. In the late fifties I got an idea for a story I wanted to do on cloning. Periodically over the next few decades, I thought of the idea but never developed it into a story. Fortunately for me, cloning became fact rather than fiction, lending more authenticity to my tale, "Each Man in His Time," written thirty years after I began to think about the idea!

On the other hand, I started "Whose Woods These Are" with only the vague notion of wanting to place a story on my grandfather's farm in Pennsylvania. I sat down at my computer and simply let a story pour forth.

You never know when an idea will strike nor how long it will take to develop. But if you want to be a teller of original tales, you have to be prepared for that time, whenever it is.

Three

Creating Characters

A story is a narrative that sets up and then resolves or brings to completion a circumstance or series of circumstances. All stories in some way create anticipation or suspense. The listener or reader of a story should want to know the outcome.

The most concise example of a story is a joke. Unless it's a "shaggy dog" type, it most often is cut of all extraneous matter. Only what is necessary to the telling is included. Often a great deal is implied.

Aristotle once wrote that a play has a beginning, a middle, and an end. Since theatre is a kind of storytelling, the same idea can be applied to all stories. They are complete in themselves. They include anything necessary to their understanding.

Stories have central ideas or themes. Generally, in a story, as opposed to a full-length play or a novel, there are fewer themes.

Many stories contain plots. That is, the action builds to a climax. Yet, this is not a necessary ingredient of all stories. Folk tales and parables often do not have this sort of action line but rather are thematic in structure.

Yet we cannot have any of these things without one essential ingredient, a central character, which in most cases is a human being, though it does not necessarily have to be.

The Importance of Characterization

Characterization is one of the most important aspects of a story. It is the primary means of developing the plot and of stating the theme. The type of character often determines the environment. Even the situation is to a large extent determined by the characters since any person placed in a specific set of circumstances will react to those circumstances in a different way than anyone else will. In the following from "The Mad Countess," written by Mary Louise O'Hara, the character comes across clearly.

> At the Versailles Court of Louis the Fourteenth, King of France, the newly wed countess had become an oddity. Courtiers were whispering—when the king or his favorites could not hear—that she must be mad, completely mad.
>
> Elise, the dainty little countess, was painting pictures of onions! Large, small, yellow, pearly, and scallions with long green stems, and she nibbled them constantly.
>
> She sat at an easel in her elegant room, slender fingers, and taffeta gown smudged with charcoal. She drew composition after composition and then painted them slowly.
>
> Elise was the daughter of a renowned scholar, poor but of noble lineage. Their estate lay far from Versailles, but news of Elise's beauty had reached the king's ear, ever sensitive to feminine allurement.

He invited her to enjoy his court and although
her father needed her to help with translations, the
king's wish was always a command.
To Louis' delight she charmed everyone—
especially him—with her wit and grace, unexpected
in such a young and beautiful girl.

Although we do not yet know Elise because we have
only heard about her, we can easily become intrigued
by her. We can become involved with her.

Character is that element of a story with which the
audience most closely identifies. There are exceptions.
In some stories, character is deemphasized and audiences empathize with the plight of an entire group of
people or with a social condition. But in most stories it
is the character as an individual for whom the reader
or listener feels empathy or sympathy.

Quite often ideas for a story come from choosing and
developing a character. Suppose the person who
comes to mind is self-centered. This will probably
make you think of a situation in which to place this
person so the selfishness can be revealed. Next you'll
choose other characters with whom the central figure
can react. The situations suggest the conflict, from
which the remaining elements of the story can be
developed.

Knowing Your Characters

None of us knows how we will react to a new situation. We can only guess. The same is true of the characters. Still, you should know how they are *likely* to
react. What will cause them to flare up or back down?
If they are threatened, will they retreat or will they
fight?

The more planning you do before the writing
begins, the better. It helps to know much more about a

character than you'll ever reveal in the story. Characterization can be compared to a building that has many sub-levels. Only a small part is visible, just as in life only a small part of a person's psychological makeup is revealed to others. A large portion is buried below the surface, but there is a depth from which to draw. Because of a character's background and experiences, he or she will react believably, but differently from another character in any situation.

In reading the following excerpt from Richard Stone's "Messages," you can immediately sense the depth of the character. Although she isn't doing much, you infer what she's like on various levels. More than many stories, "Messages" is a character study, and we learn about the character by seeing her reactions to what goes on around her.

> Ellen Chavez waited. They had put her on the sixteenth floor this year, and while she enjoyed the view of the Alameda from her window, she did not appreciate the seemingly interminable waits for the elevators. True, she could use the service stairs, but they exited through the kitchen, and she found the transit unappealing. Still, she was hardy enough now to do so, and in fact, had done so when the elevators were out of service the second day after her arrival. However, she enjoyed watching the people and listening to their conversations. It appealed to her sense of the ridiculous when the elevators seemed to take on a life of their own, refusing to obey the electric impulses, stopping first at one wrong floor, then another, before finally settling to the lobby. She regarded such trips as mild adventures, and when the other passengers' fears would threaten to turn to panic she would reassure them that such behavior was the result of

the earthquake that year, and that while the
machines were erratic, they were, nonetheless safe.

Besides what is stated about Mrs. Chavez, you can
infer that she obviously has been ill or incapacitated.
This can be seen in "she was hardy enough now to do
so." This is an illustration of saying something "between" the lines. It makes the reader or listener
wonder why she apparently wasn't hardy earlier.

You can see that she is level-headed. She views as
"mild adventures" things that panic others. By seeing
the character in action, even though it is a mild sort of
action, you can begin to learn things about her. This is
the beginning of the story. As yet, you do not know
Mrs. Chavez's physical characteristics nor vital statis-
tics. The story is a gradual unfolding of her personality.

Once characters in a story are developed, they often
take the action into their own hands. To force them to
go any way other than the direction they themselves
take may come across as artificial. By allowing them to
speak for themselves, you may receive some surprises.
But if you examine their psychological basis and background, you should discover that they acted logically,
even though unexpectedly. In my story, "Whose
Woods These Are," at the beginning the character is
thinking of buying out an electronics firm simply because he has a need to appear powerful. I thought that
at the end he would decide not to buy it. But he himself had different ideas. In effect, he told me: "Why
shouldn't I buy it? I have the money. Maybe I did let
go of some of my feelings, but it would be fun to own
the firm, not because I need to now but simply because
I want to." So I let the character have his own way.

This is not a mystical sort of thing, though it may seem so. When you are deeply involved with a character, he or she does take on a personality and become real to you.

You can't know everything about a character immediately, just as it is a slow process to learn to know someone in real life. Certainly, you form first impressions of people, but these impressions often aren't lasting.

I mentioned that with "Whose Woods These Are" I sat down and simply wrote. Yet, the story went through many revisions. I believe the reason was that I didn't beforehand analyze and get to know my character. It was only as I wrote that he became real, that, in effect, he revealed himself to me.

Character Analysis

There are five broad categories of character analysis: 1) physical characteristics, 2) background, 3) attitude and beliefs, 4) patterns of behavior, and 5) dominant traits. All of these are related and affect a character's attitude and behavior.

When analyzing a character, one of the first things to figure out is physical attributes such as height, weight, eye color, and any distinguishing features. Then you try to determine what makes the character an individual, different from others of the same general type. Obviously, the physical appearance over which a character has some control—for instance, hair style, clothing, and makeup—will follow a certain pattern because of the character's feelings and attitudes about life.

It also helps to know the characters' backgrounds. Where did they grow up? Were their families poor? Rich? How did the economic situation affect their outlook? How much schooling have they had? What are their interests and hobbies? What kind of work do theydo? Are they happy with their jobs?

What sort of speech pattern do they have? Is it affected by the location where they grew up, by their schooling, or by their present environment? How does their speech reflect their personalities? What is their vocal quality?

Would others like them? Why, or why not? What were the biggest influences in their lives? What in their backgrounds has caused the biggest changes in their outlook? Are they optimistic or pessimistic? Introverted or extroverted?

What beliefs and attitudes do they hold? What brought about these beliefs and attitudes? How did parental attitudes, habits, living conditions, and environment affect them? Do they like other people?

What are their dominant traits? Are they moral persons? What do they hope to accomplish in life? All the questions will not be answered directly in the story, but they will allow you to know and project your character as a three-dimensional individual. You can introduce much of the pertinent information into the exposition.

All of the major or leading characters can be analyzed using the questions mentioned above and any other questions you think are important. Then you can examine the relationships among the characters. What do they think and feel about each other? How do they react with each other? In "Whose Woods These Are," Roy tends to be a loner, except that he and his wife are very close.

To make the characters credible it helps to understand what motivates them. In "Whose Woods These Are," Roy's motivating force was his need not to show any weakness. It's easy to empathize with him because almost everyone, as a kid, looks upon parents as powerful and omniscient.

Of course, creating characters is a subjective process. The things you write are your perceptions of the world. They show how you feel and what you believe.

Often our characters are different parts of ourselves. Each human being has the basis or potential for developing nearly every personality trait. Others may have talents in areas we do not, or abilities to do things we cannot do. Still, we relate to others. But if we could go back and arrange a different set of circumstances for our early lives, we probably would be totally different people. Thus, there are bits of everyone's character traits in us, and bits of our traits in everyone else. We aren't all murderers or potential murderers, but in certain circumstances most of us could be, if our families were threatened, for instance. But more than that, even murderers have some positive traits. They have some characteristics with which we can sympathize or identify. It's up to you to find these traits in your characters and then to portray them.

After developing your main characters, you need to decide what traits of those characters you want to bring to the listener, which facets of their personalities are important for understanding the story. Even though you know your central characters fully, the audience doesn't or can't. There just isn't time. And so the major characters have to appear simpler than people in real life so the audience can easily grasp what they are like. This can be done through exaggeration and pointing up important facets of their personalities. In developing a story you are limited to the amount of time you can take to tell it, maybe ten or twenty minutes. This means you can concentrate on only a limited number of personality traits. If you try to show too much about a character, he or she may come across as vague rather than as being well-developed.

Often it's a good idea to think of your characters in terms of goals or drives. What does each want the most, at least at the time you are presenting them in a story? For instance, in Jack London's "To Build a Fire," the characters' goal is to make a fire so he won't freeze to death. At other times in his life, the character would have had other goals.

Generally, the conflict of a story deals with the character attempting to reach this goal. There may be secondary goals, but if they become too important, again the audience may be confused. Of course, the story will deal mainly with the protagonist's struggles to reach a goal. But other characters also have needs and wants. If the antagonist is a person, his or her drives are directly opposite the protagonist's.

Determining the Dominant Traits

The following is excerpted from a story called "Love So Amazing, So Divine" by Amy Belding Brown. The character's dominant trait is her infatuation. It becomes clearer as the story progresses that Elizabeth has romanticized David Ellis to the point of obsession. So this is what the story deals with. Certainly, in other circumstances she would have other important traits. But they would be extraneous to this story.

> Elizabeth knew that the preacher watched her during his sermons. She felt his hot, blue eyes on her, raking the skin of her face; they penetrated her like nails. Sometimes she hardly listened to his words at all. His voice was like a trumpet above her; she heard notes, felt them pour over her, but

she made no attempt to understand. It seemed enough to sit there under his gaze, bathed in the energy of his devotion to the Lord. She left worship services cleansed and weakened, barely able to speak.

Type versus Individual

Because no character is entirely alien to us, each has common traits. Each then, to a degree, is a type. More than that, your characters need to be typified to a certain extent for the reader or listener to able to identify with them. Since characterization cannot be fully revealed in the length of a story, the listener needs to be able to assume some things. If the audience members see someone who appears to be of a type with whom they can identify, they will have no trouble in assuming certain things about the person. You don't then have to express them openly. The audience can safely assume that a typical mother and father would be concerned about their children. On the other hand, if the major characters don't have distinctive traits of their own, things that set them apart from others, the story hasn't made them believable. There has to be a balance between typification and individuality.

When characters are opposed in any way, we learn more about their emotional and psychological characteristics. We can tell a lot about them by what they do when opposed. Their reactions to crisis or conflict may reveal things they may not even know about themselves. When the opposition becomes the strongest, the most important qualities of the character will be revealed. One of the best ways to hold listeners' attention is to make them want to know how a character will respond to a particular set of circumstances.

Revealing Character

It's a common misconception that the central character has to undergo a massive change or a personality reversal. Such a change isn't logical. Personality has been determined by a human being's entire background, so it's not reasonable that one major crisis should cause someone to reject all that has gone before and undergo complete psychological and emotional change.

Instead, we have character revelation. A part of a character's personality that wasn't apparent previously is revealed. The revelation occurs gradually throughout the story. If the listeners were to see the total character at the beginning, they probably would have little interest in the outcome. Any revelation must be logical in view of personality and background.

In reading this excerpt from "The Pleiades," by Jerine P. Watson-Miner, we only gradually learn who and what the characters are and what they hope to accomplish.

> They were five, gathered together. And they waited. Soft, muted sobs escaped from them now and again, and they occasionally dabbed at their moist redness with small, white cottony balls.
>
> Shutter couldn't sit still. She kept lifting her feet, one after the other, and wringing two of her hands. Her nervous agitation irritated her sisters and her constant movement made the floor tremble.

Little by little, character traits are revealed as the story progresses. Although you can see that the characters probably are not human beings, the author doesn't let you know until you're well into the story that the five characters are black widow spiders, seeking revenge for the killing of their sister by a farm wife.

Characters may change their minds or their courses of action or even their goals. But such changes are brought about by something already inherent in their personalities. The changes result only from seeds already growing and that maybe even the characters themselves failed to recognize. It's often been said that adversity best shows a person's true makeup. When faced with trouble, the strong often become weak and the weak become strong.

Even if a character is defeated, even if the person commits suicide or is driven insane, the potential for that happening must be there before the event actually occurs.

Determining the Outcome

The climax of any good story must be a logical outcome not only of what has happened previously, but also of what is an inherent part of the major character's makeup. Since an audience often is aware of what the ending of a story will be, the real suspense is concerned with how this outcome will be achieved, how the characters will either win or lose.

When beginning to develop a story, it's a good idea to try to decide what situations will best reveal the dominant traits of your characters. For example, if a man has an overwhelming drive to succeed at his job, he can be placed in a situation where this drive can be tested. Suppose he has a chance for a promotion, but two of his co-workers have the same chance. How does this affect him? How does he act with the co-workers, with his family, and with his boss? Put him in situations with each of them and find out.

How does he react to his wife's accusations that he's spending too much time at the office to the detriment of his family? How does he react differently when the issue of overtime comes up again during a conversation with his boss? How does he treat his co-workers? We must see him in the situations to know the answers.

Seeds for any important action have to be planted ahead of time, or the listener feels cheated. The characters not only speak to themselves but also foresee situations in which they may later be placed.

Jerine Watson-Miner showed early on that the characters were greatly disturbed, so it comes as no surprise that their goal is to avenge the death of their sister. Given the framework of the story and the idea that the spiders possess human characteristics, they behave logically in deciding to kill the woman, although they previously considered her a friend. They plot out in great detail how they will reach their goal and then carry out the actions they've decided on.

Characters in a story have to control the action. The plot cannot be imposed upon them, or the action will become artificial. The character wants something, and the play is the story of his or her efforts to get it. The story should reach as quickly as possible from the introduction to the conflict to the climax.

Four

Plotting Your Story

From the time we are small, we learn to like stories. When we think of them, we generally think first of being entertained and second, maybe, of learning something. Stories are interesting because they usually deal with people in situations with which we can identify. Our interest is held because of a story's unfolding and its revelations. In other words, the plot keeps us in suspense.

Definition of Plot

A plot involves the meeting of opposing forces. Their struggle continues until one of them is overcome. One force is the protagonist; the other the antagonist. The former is the person who needs or wants something; the antagonist opposes him or her. The protagonist generally is an individual, though in rare cases it can be a group. The antagonist is another person, a group, or a non-individualized force such as social or economic conditions. It may be the protagonist's environment, the forces of nature, or even a condition within the mind that is shown largely in the central character's relationships with others.

A story begins with a particular situation in which there has been balance, or else the balance has been upset shortly before the action begins. At any rate, until the beginning of the action there has been no great difficulty for the characters. Then the **inciting incident** occurs and the balance is destroyed. A question is raised that must be answered. This introduces the **rising action**. During this period, the protagonist's problem is intensified through a series of complications. The suspense increases. Will the protagonist finally triumph or be defeated? The suspense, the struggle, and the conflict continue to build until the action can go no further without something irrevocable happening. This means the **turning point** of the story has been reached. Now the protagonist knows he or she will win the struggle against all opposition or else be destroyed. The actual point at which the central character wins or loses is the **climax**. The remainder of the story is devoted to the **falling action**.

Turning Point and Climax

Sometimes the turning point and the climax are the same; at other times they are separated. Suppose two men are opposed. They have been fighting with each other because one man, the antagonist, has threatened the protagonist's family. After attempting to reason with the antagonist to no avail, the protagonist decides that the only solution is to kill him. The point at which the decision is made is the turning point. The actual killing is the climax. If the decision is carried out instantaneously, the turning point and the climax are the same. If the protagonist decides to kill the antagonist but feels it would be better to wait until a more opportune time, the turning point and the climax are separated.

In most stories, except those that are very short, the action does not build in a straight line to the climax and then fall off for the unraveling or the reestablishment of the status quo. Instead, the plot involves a jagged line where a series of minor crises and struggles are introduced as part of the overall problem. Sometimes these minor problems seemingly are resolved, only to intrude again and complicate the rising action.

In the story "Giantess," by Mimi Albert, a woman plans to escape the institution in which she has been placed. She wants to live free. She does escape, but then is stopped by two policemen. The one who seems to her to be the kinder of the two takes her to the park where he lets her out. So again she has escaped. Yet, people make fun of her there as they do everywhere, and she doesn't fit in. Her problem only continues. Now, however, it is intensified because not only is she a misfit, but she has no way of living on her own. After she is pushed out:

> Stunned, I sit down on a bench, too tired even to be frightened of muggers or thieves, wishing only that I could break into the zoo to steal peanuts from the elephants. I sit in darkness, waiting for something I don't understand. I watch the lights turn as the city night begins. Suddenly a bunch of little boys runs up over a rock cliff behind my bench, smoking and swapping jokes to keep themselves brave in the dark.
>
> "What's that?" one of them says, looking at me. For a minute, as I get to my feet, I remember the boys who threw rocks at me when I was young. I'm afraid. But they stare at me and then begin to run,

and as they go, I can hear them screaming, "Frankenstein, Frankenstein," again and again like a battle cry or a warning.

"You mean Frankenstein's Monster," I say out loud but too low for them to hear. Anyway, they're gone. Suddenly tears are in my eyes and running down my face, but the tears mean only one thing, self-pity, and that's no good, so I brush them away and, bending, pick up a lit cigarette that one of them dropped and smoke it to cut down hunger. I am a city vagrant now. And it was worth it, I think again...

"You weren't missed. Where were you?" Sylvia says, when I limp into our shared room late that night. "Honey" or "Dear" they call me here. No one knows me as Miranda.

The story is not just about the problem of escaping and living on one's own. It has to do with acceptance and self-reliance. The "giantess" doesn't so much want to escape the hospital as she does to escape the kind of life that has been forced upon her. She wants acceptance, which most of the world will not give her.

The complications in all but the simplest of stories result in a series of minor climaxes, which could be compared to a fencing match. First, one person attacks and drives back the other; then the second attacks and drives back the first, over and over again at increasing intensity until one is declared the victor. Each of these minor crises somewhat alters the direction of the story. Each is introduced by one minor climax or resolution and ended by another. But the frenzy or suspense continues to build.

Even in scenes where there appears to be no conflict, it is inherent; it relates to what already has been shown. Suppose a woman is having trouble at work. She is afraid of being fired even though she is the best worker on the job. Another worker tries to degrade everything she does and tries to take credit for everything worthwhile, thus making the woman look bad in the eyes of her boss. The woman comes into direct conflict with the villain at work. At home the situation appears to be calmer. Perhaps in discussing the situation with her husband, she decides what to do. The listener knows the conflict is present, that it's inherent in the action. It comes across indirectly in what the woman says and does.

Such a scene can show a part of the woman's character not apparent in her scenes with co-workers. It may reveal more about what she thinks and thus let the audience know more about her. Since it also can show what she is planning to do, it builds suspense or anticipation.

Forward Progression

Plot refers to forward movement or progression and to action. Without some sort of forward movement, there would be little in a story to hold the listeners' interest. Action is what gives the story its life. There can be physical movement with no forward action, but such an episode leads nowhere. Conversely, there can be dramatic action without physical movement. Such action is related to the opposition of the protagonist and the antagonist in moving the story forward. It needs to be motivated by what has preceded it in the story. Much of this sort of thing occurs in "Whose Woods These Are" where the central character is remembering what occurred as he walks over his grandfather's farm.

I don't mean to imply that movement must be restricted in any way simply because it does not seem to contribute to the overall plot. Maybe it accomplishes another valid purpose that indirectly helps to advance the plot. Often, relationships or character traits important to the story can be revealed by including particular scenes, such as the brief scene between Roy and his wife in "Whose Woods These Are." We learn both that he and his wife have a good relationship and also that he is unsure of himself, rather than being all-powerful.

Often a character is individualized by some repeated action or trait. This is valid in that it helps the listener to know the character better. It's an outward sign of an emotion or trait, whose establishment may be important to the later action. For instance, it should come as no surprise that a character continually fascinated by guns eventually shoots either himself or someone else.

Action must relate in some way to the central character. Even if this person isn't present, it has to concern or be initiated because of him or her. Once characters act, they will be affected by their behavior. Forward action involves a clash of forces and is always reciprocal. It can be compared to communication. If you say hello to someone, that person usually says hello to you. If you argue with a friend, you can expect an argument back. Even in talking to a group of people in a formal situation, you receive feedback in the form of facial expression and body language. The same thing occurs among characters in a story. For every action there is reaction if the story is well-constructed.

Without dramatic action always occurring in the present tense, there would be no story. In "Whose Woods These Are" the present is strongly influenced by the past, yet the story occurs in the present. Even though Roy has built his life largely on a past incident, what he does about it in the present interests us. He decides to return home. Once there, he goes to the farm and retraces the path he, his father, and his cousin took. Yet, this is a "reliving" that occurs in the present.

Plot is the arrangement of the dramatic action to build suspense and to reach a point of no return. Each scene of action may be a few lines or a few pages. When a climax is reached or an obstacle surmounted, a new situation is introduced. For example, a man is trapped in a burning building. He is first of all confronted by a door that won't open. When he manages to get the hinges off the door, he runs into the hallway where he is met by a wall of flame. He runs back into the room, grabs a blanket, wraps it around himself, and rushes through the flames. Next he finds that the floor is crumbling beneath him, and so on. Although each problem is met and overcome, a new and worse one is introduced until the man either escapes or is overcome by the smoke and flames.

Falling Action

After the climax should come the falling action, that part of the story that shows the results of what has gone before. The climax begins to show the answer to the question asked when the problem was introduced; the falling action finishes answering the question. It may answer more fully how and why a certain thing happened. It may show the effects of the resolution on the characters. At any rate, it ties up all the loose ends. The central character should be totally responsible for the specific outcome. For example, in "Whose Woods These Are" we know that Roy has resolved his feelings. The falling action shows how he is likely to continue with his life. Here, the falling action consists of only the final paragraph.

Or to take a different sort of example: a man becomes separated from his family during wartime. The separation is the inciting incident. As soon as he is able, he begins searching for his wife and daughters. It may take years of following false leads. Throughout the action, the audience member experiences the man's fears, his apprehensions, his despair, and the fruitless bursts of hope. Finally, the man discovers a promising clue and follows through with it. It leads to the climax, finding his family. He rushes to the house where they are staying and flings open the door. The problem has been resolved and the action completed. But since the audience has suffered with the man, they want to rejoice with him. It would be insensitive to end the story at this point; it would be cheating the audience members.

Types of Conflict

There are five different types of opposition a central character in a story can encounter. They are the protagonist against: 1) another person, 2) self, 3) society, 4) nature, and 5) fate.

The most important consideration is how the character reacts to the opposition.

An example of the first type is from my story "Going Steady." The opening paragraphs define the situation.

> Martin had a gold pocket watch that had belonged to Grandma Schmidt's great, great uncle. One day in eighth-grade history, Mr. Purlman asked the class to bring in the oldest objects they could find. He said they'd talk about them and try to relate them to the past. Martin brought in the watch which Grandma Schmidt had given him on his tenth birthday.

46

That afternoon, just before the dismissal bell, Karen Sorge passed Martin a note asking if he'd let her see it.

He gives in and passes the watch to her. It is just before time for the dismissal bell. Karen's row is dismissed before Martin's, and she leaves with the watch. Martin learns that she has shown it to her friends and told them it means she and Martin are going steady. Here's is what happens the following morning in the cloakroom.

"I want my watch back, Karen."

"I don't have it."

"What!"

"I gave it to Millie to look at."

"You had no right to do that."

"You'll get your precious watch back."

"Well, I'd better." She turned away. "Karen!" he said. She faced him. "Why did you tell the other kids we're going together?"

A blush covered her face and neck. "It's none of your business."

"I want you to tell them it isn't true."

"Tell them yourself." She strode toward the doorway.

He grabbed her arm and spun her around. "You'd better tell them today, and you'd better give my watch back!" He held tight to her arm.

She jerked away. "Let me go, you..." She called him a very bad name.

Almost without thought, Martin slapped her across the cheek. Horrified, he dropped his hand. He'd never hit a girl before.

"I hate you, Martin O'Jenkins!" she screamed. "I hate you! I hate you!" She turned and ran from the room.

Often, a story that pits one person against another can easily lack depth because the struggle is all on the surface. To make it more interesting, you should probe the central character's reasons for the conflict.

The second type of conflict, a person against self, is illustrated by "Whose Woods These Are." Although it can possibly be argued that Donald created the conflict, the boy's reactions all take place inside his mind. He has never resolved the situation, but has carried it with him into middle age.

The third type of conflict is apparent in "Giantess," where society has reacted against a human being, first when she is a child, and later when she's an adult because in her own words: "...I'm almost seven feet tall and broad to match. My skull keeps growing and my nose and forehead are so thick you can hardly see my eyes, which gives me a dull and stupid look. But I am not dull."

After her mother dies, Miranda, the giantess, is placed in a hospital:

> I cried then, huge tears splashing down my cheeks. It was social workers to whom I wept. Doctors. Psychologists. I might as well have kept my eyes dry...They didn't say that nobody would want to have me in their house. Nobody would want to work next to me in a factory. They didn't say it. But I knew.

People or society in general made fun of Miranda, treating her like an animal with no feelings. Another example of this type of conflict, of course, is "Johnny and the Monster." The society or environment into which Johnny has moved thinks he's different and won't accept him.

An excellent example of a human being against nature is London's "To Build a Fire." Often, this type of plot is difficult to write in that it comes across as too melodramatic. Many times in stories that pit a person against a force of nature, the conflict only superficially is between the protagonist and the force. Often it's the man or woman against self in the reaction to the flood or drought.

The fifth type of opposition, a person against fate, is equally difficult to make convincing in that it often comes across as the protagonist's being controlled by fate without any sense of freedom. Often, in a story that has this type of conflict, we also see the character struggling with self over what to do in reaction to fate. In a sense, Miranda's struggle in "Giantess" was brought about by fate, the death of her mother. But this was only a point along the way in her continuing struggle against society.

An example of a protagonist in conflict with fate is my story "Charity" in which the boy's father has been badly injured in a coal mining accident, and the mother simply cannot provide the necessities for herself and her son:

> Mama was too proud to go to the union hall for the free cheese when the miners were on strike. "My family has never taken charity," she said. That's why I was surprised when she let me go for the "treat" that was passed out before Christmas.
>
> It didn't amount to much, but Mama said I better appreciate it because it was all I'd get. It wasn't a threat; it was a simple statement of fact.
>
> The miners had been on strike. Then when they went back to work, a loaded coal car jumped the track and pinned Daddy against the wall...Daddy's

legs were crushed. The doctor couldn't do anything except cut them off.

Structuring the Scenes

Each scene should follow the same structure that the story as a whole does. That means there is an inciting incident or a change of some sort in the direction of the action until this particular complication is solved. An example is when the giantess has difficulty with the police. This is a minor complication, within the overall plot, but it has an inciting incident. She falls and the police come to see why.

In a story with a plot a scene or episode can be thought of as a motivational unit, in which the protagonist has a goal he or she has to achieve. To go back to the analogy of the burning building, each new scene would occur when the circumstances changed. There is the matter of opening the door, escaping through the hallway, and so forth. They all contribute to the major goal of getting away from the building, but each is slightly different.

A crisis should continue to build, and the climax should be inevitable yet somewhat unexpected. This does not mean there has to be a surprise ending such as O'Henry used. Rather, there needs to be a twist or twists that show *how* the climax is reached, even if we know from the type of story and the content how the problem will be resolved.

Generally, you'll want to write a story with a simple plot, one that is easy to follow. The listening audience does not have the advantage of the reader in being able to reread or look back over the material to find something they missed. You'll also want to include only those characters necessary to telling the story and making it entertaining.

Five

Making Your Story Believable

A good story has tension, a "looking forward." It grows out of the situation and the interplay of the characters with themselves, the situation, or other characters.

Conflict often is equated with tension, yet tension can be provided through suspense, through wanting to know the story's outcome.

Tension often is the result of highly emotional scenes, a stretching forward to a specific goal that will be reached as a result of the emotional encounter.

Foreshadowing

Tension often involves foreshadowing, a device used by a storyteller or writer to suggest that something of importance will happen later that will affect the characters and the outcome.

In "Giantess" there is tension throughout because the audience knows that Miranda cannot quietly accept her "fate." Rather, she has struggled all her life against it.

Even though the inciting incident—the death of the husband—in "Song of the Dog" occurs before the story begins, there is tension throughout because the reader or listener wants to know how Kazu will handle her grief. Her struggle then is against the grief. A story that contained nothing momentous wouldn't hold anyone's attention.

In a way, these two stories have foreshadowing in the sense of anticipation you feel in hearing or reading them. But more obvious foreshadowing involves deliberately tantalizing the reader or listener by hinting that something is going to happen. Of course, then the storyteller has to deliver; whatever is hinted at has to occur. The foreshadowing can be something as obvious as: "Although he had nothing to pin it on, Ron Evans was certain that his partner was in big trouble." Of course, the listener should wonder what the trouble is and how it will affect Ron Evans.

Consider: "I am a sentient. And I am afraid" (David F. Hamilton and Peter W. Telep, "Pathosphere"). Near the beginning of the story, these lines make the reader wonder who is afraid and why. They set up a situation that will follow.

Here's the opening paragraph of "Maps," by Michael Langley:

> This room looks much different than it did when it was mine. The bed is by the door now, instead of against the wall and the shelves are filled with souvenirs—stamps, matchbooks, shotglasses— instead of my books and tennis magazines. Old maps in cardboard boxes cover the floor near the door so I have to step over them to get in. I wonder where to start clearing out. Here on the shelf is the little plastic dolphin my brother bought at Sea World five years ago.

This also is a kind of foreshadowing since by stating that "the room looks much different," the narrator is promising to explain why and what has happened. Then he says, "I wonder where to start clearing it out," which should make the reader want to know why it is going to be cleared out. Is the character, the narrator, moving back in or what?

Foreshadowing involves revealing character traits that are important to some later action. You hear a story in which one of the characters exhibits violent anger over a minor incident. Later, you are not taken off guard when he goes into a rage and kills someone.

It is important to remember that every clue you plant, every detail of characterization that is planted early on, should be important further into the story. There is no reason to make someone selfish, for example, if the trait is then dropped.

Influences and Goals

Even though a story should occur in the present, the characters were not born just at the moment the story begins. They are influenced by the past. A good way to think of any important character is that the person is *pushed by the past and pulled by the future so that he or she continually moves forward in the present.*

Relate this to yourself. Because of certain experiences in your background, you behave in a certain way. Because of the jujitsu incident in "Whose Woods These Are," Roy is influenced (pushed) in striving toward his goal (which is pulling him forward).

Often, of course, stories contain flashbacks. There are two important points to remember here. First, a flashback should be included only when necessary to reveal character and show how and why a person is influenced in any particular way. Second, the flashback also should occur in the "present." Think of this as watching a historical film. You are asked to believe that what has happened perhaps hundreds of years ago is occurring in the present.

The same is true of flashbacks. You are asked to believe that you have left one "present," involving the forward movement of the plot, and gone to another "present," which is included only to explain the actions of the plot. There are also "thinkbacks," when a character doesn't actually return to the past in a flashback but returns only in his or her memory.

Although at first glance it may seem that "Whose Woods These Are" contains a flashback, it does not. You can tell this from the following: "Then like the boy I remembered, I started to walk up through the fields, beside the bank of the stream. Along the way I thought of that other walk, became for a time that long-ago boy." But this occurred only in memory, as evidenced by: "The day was fresh then..." Not *now*, but *then* the day was fresh. In effect, the central character, Roy, is narrating and remembering the past, not entering it.

Dialogue

Dialogue has to be both natural and appropriate to the character and the situation, as well as be clear to the listener. How can you know what is natural to your character?

The dialogue has to fit a character's personality. If people are stuffy, they will speak in a more formal, stilted manner than will uninhibited outgoing people, even though the same nuances of dialect may be present in the speech of both. Not only should the dialogue be consistent, but it should help reveal character.

When you hear a stranger speak for the first time, you can tell many things about him or her. In other words, the person speaks to you nonverbally, through word choice, sentence structure, and so on. A timid person might answer hesitantly, in single syllables, while looking off into the distance.

A good test in a story is to tell it to someone else, without the dialogue tags like "John said" or "She answered." If you've done a good job in delineating character and having the people speak in a characteristic manner, the listener should be able to tell who is speaking, even without the names being given.

Environment determines in part the way a character speaks. Many American-born residents of New York's Chinatown speak English with a Chinese accent. This is natural because they imitate the speech patterns of parents and relatives. A northerner may move to the south and soon develop aspects of southern dialect. The way a character speaks can tell us about ethnic or regional background.

The extent of one's schooling often determines certain speech habits. Even the type of schooling affects speech. A computer hack would talk differently than a swimming coach, even though they have the same amount of formal education.

Dialogue also helps show emotion, not just by the words but by the speech patterns. People experiencing strong or violent emotions tend to speak in a choppier manner than they would when relaxed or happy. All of this is important to remember to make your stories sound true to life.

Frame of Reference

What makes a story seem real? Why are we willing to accept a world in which there is intergalactic travel or where a nuclear holocaust has destroyed most of the world?

It has to do with establishing a "logical" frame of reference. This means that the storyteller creates a world that, although different from the one we inhabit, is consistent. It has certain natural laws, inhabitants, and physical characteristics that remain the same throughout the story.

When this is the case, the audience is willing, as the poet and critic Samuel Taylor Coleridge suggested, to suspend their disbelief. They are willing to accept almost anything if a frame of reference is created in which these things can exist.

If you create a world in which magic exists, it must exist throughout the story. (Of course, sorcerers may lose their "magic touch" and so on, but magic still must be a reality).

It is only when elements of the story contradict the created world or the frame of reference that they become unacceptable or unbelievable. If intergalactic travel has not been established at the beginning of the story, or at least the possibility of its development in the near future, you cannot at the end have your protagonist suddenly hop on a starship and zoom off to faraway places. Part of this is what was meant by foreshadowing. The possibility of anything of importance occurring has to be stated or implied before it actually does occur.

In "Song of the Dog," Kazu's husband could not logically come back to life, although resurrection is possible in other stories where the framework is established. Miranda in "Giantess" could not logically become a normal-looking being in the framework of the story. Yet, stories are written where miracles of this sort occur. But the possibility of such occurrences must be woven into the exposition. You have to be selective in the type of universe you want to create and then stick to it throughout.

Selectivity

Along the same lines, everything connected with the story needs to be selective. It would be impossible to present every detail of a character, a scene of dialogue, or a world in a long novel, let alone a story, particularly one that is to be told.

Throughout, you present bits and pieces, and the listener takes them and adds his or her own experience and expectations to them. An action that would take longer in life can be compressed and heightened. Time can be condensed. Things can be accomplished more quickly and sentences formulated into a better structure in a story, while still appearing or sounding natural.

Probably the most remembered element from the majority of stories is characterization. We often think we know a character well and that the person is well-rounded and three dimensional. But if we stop to analyze this feeling and go back through a story, we find that actually few traits were actually mentioned or portrayed, and most of them were dealt with only in passing.

The same is true of events and situations. Generally, they are painted in broad strokes only, and the listener is willing to fill in the details. If you describe a house or another location, your listener probably will visualize it. Yet, if the listener and you had the ability to paint a realistic picture of what was described, the two paintings would be quite different.

It would bog the story down to include too many details, and it would be confusing as well.

Dialogue also has to be selective. It shouldn't contain the hesitations and false starts common in conversation. Neither should it change direction or ramble, unless for a specific purpose such as delineating character. By its very nature, a short story has to be condensed, so every line and every word of dialogue must have meaning.

A story is selective in that it should begin as near the climax as possible, often presenting background material as dialogue, flashback, or memory. If a scene isn't absolutely necessary to the development of the plot, it need not be included.

Plot versus Story

So far you've been reading about both "story" and "plot," which you may think are the same. They aren't. Plot, as you know, is the action of the story. It includes the inciting incident, the rising action, the turning point, climax, and the falling action. In this sense it is very rigid, detailing only what happens from the time the balance is upset until the problem is resolved.

"Story" on the other hand includes much more. A story usually begins earlier than the plot. In "Whose Woods These Are" the story started years before, during the time of World War II. The plot only begins with the central character deciding to do something about what happened back then.

Kazu's story includes her entire culture and how it treats death, as well as being her individual story. And as noted, even the inciting incident began prior to the opening lines of the story.

The term "story" is all-encompassing, supposing that an entire fictional world exists in which there may be a multiplicity of events, people, backgrounds, and so forth that bear directly on the stretching forward.

You need to remember that although you can record what occurs to you during a single hour of your life, you did exist before this, and you and your world will exist beyond this brief time. The same is true of a story. The characters, situations, and events do not exist completely in a vacuum. But when developing the story, you select only those events that have bearing on your plot.

The purpose is to get the protagonist and hence the listener from Point A to Point B in as direct a route as possible. You can't dawdle along the way. You can't stop to admire the scenery. You must keep your attention on reaching your goal.

The following story, told recently on PBS radio, has nothing whatsoever that is extraneous. Although told from a first person point of view, that of a brother, it is about a young woman who sacrificed her entire life for her father, even to the point of giving up her own chances at happiness. Finally, she could no longer endure, perhaps going a little insane, and took her revenge. The catalyst to her action was the fact that she and the policeman were lovers and she was expecting his child.

TONIGHT MY SISTER DANCED FREEDOM

by Marsh Cassady

Tonight my sister tied ribbons in her hair and danced in the moonlight after a lifetime of caring for our papa, Ezekiel Mills.

Old man Bowen, always spying from his window, must have called the cops.

On the porch, watching oak leaves shimmer in a ghostly glow, I heard the siren, waited for Constable Joe Dunne to come stand beside me. Immovable as pillars, we two observed Belle's dance.

Feet barely touching the fallen leaves, the dewy grass, faster and faster, she twisted, spun, wheeled, long blonde tresses floating like clouds above her shoulders.

Another kind of cloud, making me think of a veil on a new grass widow, hid the moon. All at once Belle collapsed, a heap. Hands, opposing, upside-down questions marks, lay in her lap.

Light through the window caught Joe's eyes, picturing him like a timid rabbit flushed from a brush pile. Gently, I touched my hand to his sleeve, smiled, nodded, turned.

Papa sat in his favorite chair, the smell of tobacco strong in the pipe beside him, his body covered with fish mouths, streaming red.

The cruiser's motor roared, kicked gravel, sped Joe and Belle away. Maybe they'd name the child Joseph Ezekiel, I thought. Joseph Ezekiel would be a fitting name.

Only what is necessary to the story and to the establishment of the framework, the fictional world, is included. Such descriptions as "watching oak leaves shimmer in a ghostly glow" and "another kind of cloud, making me think of a veil on a new grass widow, hid the moon" help create the mood, somewhat eerie, and the universe. It is not exactly the one with which we are familiar because few people in the present use the term "grass widow" and few women wear "veils."

Because of this, you perhaps are more willing to accept the circumstances—the father's murder and the escape with the policeman. But you have to listen or read carefully to be sure you grasp the meaning.

Six

Exposition and Description

A story should have a good hook. That means a catchy beginning, often memorized, that piques the listeners' interest and makes them want to know what is going to happen. It almost always poses questions the listener wants answered.

For example:

> "Elizabeth knew the preacher watched her during his sermons" (from "Love So Amazing, So Divine," by Amy Belding Brown).

> "There were five gathered together. And they waited" (from "The Pleiades," by Jerine Watson-Miner).

> "It was a winter sewn with the thread of pain, sewn to a tattered autumn at one end and to an as yet unshrunk spring on the other—a winter which lingered too long, so that the gray of the clouds cast musty shadows on everyone's spirit" (from "The Cup," by Joseph J. Juknialis).

"The villagers who lived around The Point didn't think Ol' Sam would stay on after Kate died" (from "Ol' Sam's Secret," by James L. Henderschedt).

If I were to hear any of these beginnings, I'd want to know more. Who is Elizabeth and why does she think the preacher is watching her? What five people are gathered? For what purpose? Why was the winter painful? Painful to whom? What was wrong with everyone that each let it affect his or her spirit?

Who are Ol' Sam and Kate? Why would the villagers expect Sam either to stay or go? What sort of relationship did Kate and Sam have? What was Sam's relationship with the villagers?

All of these stories have excellent beginnings, and all are quite different. It doesn't matter how you begin, just so your listener wants to hear more. A good way of judging this, of course, is the simple test of asking yourself if you would be interested in the story if it were told by someone else.

The idea is to give the listener information about what is going to happen, but not to give too much.

Exposition

Earlier you read about the idea of creating an entire fictional world or universe for each story. The things that make up this universe come under the heading of exposition. This includes anything the reader needs to know in order to understand the fictional world and to follow the progression of the story. It includes prior events that have bearing on what happens, given circumstances (the way things are now), personality traits and the relationship among the characters.

There are two types of exposition. The first involves only background material. The second type, the progressive exposition, is related to the changing situations and often involves character revelation. Background exposition deals with the opening situation of the story. What are the general conditions, not only of the characters but also of the world in which they exist? Where does the story take place? Is there anything the audience needs to know about that location? Is it a desolate farmhouse, easily accessible to pranksters or thieves? Is it a slum area where stepping outside can mean being assaulted and beaten? What is the condition of the city or the country? What are the prevailing attitudes of the population? What are the feelings of the time? How do the central and secondary characters' feelings mesh with what their country or the world in general believes? Such questions need to be considered if they are important to the story.

If the action takes place in another time or location, what differences are there from our own time? Are the natural laws the same as in our world and time? It's best to work the exposition into the story bit by bit to make it appear realistic. An audience doesn't want to hear just a recitation of facts, nor will they even be able to absorb these facts if they are given one after another.

Moreover, you need to work it in naturally. A conversation like the following is not logical because the characters already know these facts, and it's obvious the storyteller is simply presenting exposition the audience should know.

> "It's been three years since we moved into this house, do you realize that?" John asked.
> "Yes, just when the business started to fail, and we decided to sell out."

> "And then your brother was good enough to lend us the money to tide us over until we actually had a check from the new owners."
> "And now we think of this as the best home we've ever had."

And so on. As you see, this is nearly nonsensical in that people simply wouldn't tell each other things that they already know, unless, of course, for emphasis. Rather, the above information can be worked into the story in any number of ways that are better. One could be a flashback to the time the two characters were having difficulties and were forced to sell their business.

You could also present the information in the form of narration or introspection:

> Mary breathed deeply, a sigh of contentment. Across the street the Johnston's two kids played in their driveway. It was peaceful here, so different from the city.
> At first she'd been afraid she'd be bored, there'd be nothing to fill up her days. But she was wrong. She rarely even thought of the business anymore. Up until three years ago, it had seemed to consume her life.

You get the idea. Work the exposition in so that it bears directly on the present, the stretching forward. Generally, the exposition should concern the main characters and how the world at large affects them.

Before you begin actually developing the story, it can help to create the fictional world completely in your own mind, and then write down all the conditions that you think will have bearing on the plot. If you feel it necessary, you can then rank the expository material in the order by which it needs to be known.

This way it can be woven in more skillfully and gradually. What the audience needs to know, for instance, a third of the way through the story may not have been necessary for them to know at the beginning. The listeners shouldn't be aware that they are being given expository material, but only that the story is a complete unit within itself and that it accomplishes its aim.

Although the following is taken from a play rather than a story, it is an excellent method of presenting exposition in that the audience member learns a great deal about the characters in an entertaining way.

Instead of simply having the two characters present the facts, Oscar Wilde has them get in little digs at each other, which in turn provides conflict and tension. The excerpt is from *The Importance of Being Earnest*.

> ALGERNON: How are you, my dear Earnest? What brings you up to town?
>
> JACK: Oh, pleasure, pleasure! What else should bring one anywhere? Eating as usual, I see, Algy!
>
> ALGERNON: (Stiffly) I believe it is customary in good society to take some slight refreshment at five o'clock. Where have you been since last Thursday?
>
> JACK: (sitting down on the sofa) In the country.
>
> ALGERNON: What on earth do you do there?
>
> JACK: (pulling off his gloves) When one is in town one amuses oneself. When one is in the country one amuses other people. It is excessively boring.
>
> ALGERNON: And who are the people you amuse?
>
> JACK: (Airily) Oh, neighbors, neighbors.
>
> ALGERNON: Got nice neighbors in your part of Shropshire?
>
> JACK: Perfectly horrid! Never speak to them.

ALGERNON: How immensely you must amuse them! (Goes over and takes a sandwich) By the way, Shropshire is your county, is it not?

JACK: Eh? Shropshire? Yes, of course. Hallo! Why all these cups? Why cucumber sandwiches? Why such reckless extravagance in one so young? Who is coming to tea?

ALGERNON: Oh! merely Aunt Augusta and Gwendolen.

JACK: How perfectly delightful!

ALGERNON: Yes, that is all very well; but I am afraid Aunt Augusta won't approve of your being here.

JACK: May I ask why?

ALGERNON: My dear fellow, the way you flirt with Gwendolen is perfectly disgraceful. It is almost as bad as the way Gwendolen flirts with you.

JACK: I am in love with Gwendolen. I have come up to town expressly to propose to her.

ALGERNON: I thought you had come up for pleasure? ...I call that business.

JACK: How utterly unromantic you are!

ALGERNON: I really don't see anything romantic in proposing. It is very romantic to be in love. But there is nothing romantic about a definite proposal. Why, one may be accepted. One usually is, I believe. Then the excitement is all over. The very essence of romance is uncertainty. If ever I get married, I'll certainly try to forget the fact.

Not only is the passage amusing, but we learn a great deal about what Jack has been up to and about the relationships among the various characters, including Gwendolen.

Description

One type of exposition involves description, both of people and places. Ideally, this too should be woven into the story and given for a particular reason other than that the audience needs to know it. Description can be used to establish a mood, to create a feeling of suspense or danger, or to help the characters themselves identify a location or another person. In a told story, description often is brief, as can be seen in most folktales or myths.

Description of a place can help determine a character's personality or tastes in home, clothing, and so on. In the following excerpt from my story "Ties," you learn a little about both the location, Southern California, and the character.

> Dennis was an early riser. He liked nothing better than to watch the sun float into the sky and slowly burn the morning mist from the sea. Before the sound of traffic and the awakening city intruded on the morning, he loved to walk along the sand and rocks, listening to the scree, scree of the seagulls, the roar of the waves. When he closed his eyes, he imagined those waves to be sheets of rain, beating on the roof, as it had in his youth. It was a comforting sound, perhaps the only comforting sound he remembered.
>
> In memory's eye he saw himself huddled under thin blankets, sketching, drawing, inventing cartoon knights who would ride their white horses up the tenement stairs and carry him off.
>
> He walked along the beach now as was his daily custom. Stocky, well-built, his body hard like a boxer's, he rarely gave his physical condition a thought. When he did, he chuckled at the fact that friends often expressed envy for his having to do so little to stay in shape. He wore running shorts and T-shirts, often torn and faded, in the summer, and baggy sweats in the winter. He wore them not as a reverse kind of snobbery as people were wont to do

in a place like the Village, but because they were comfortable. He was an active man, who loved to walk and run for the joy of it. Staying in shape was merely a side benefit.

He was a physical man who loved to work with his hands, whether tinkering with a motor or touching his brush to canvas. Yet it had been so easy not to touch that brush to canvas.

In this passage you are given a great amount of exposition. And most of it is worked in for a reason that has direct bearing on the advancement of the plot.

What sorts of things do you learn? Although it's hard to separate location from conditions from character, let's try to take location first. We know it's early morning, that the location is seaside, that it's a city, that the shore consists of both sand and rock, that seagulls are flying overhead and that waves are roaring.

How about the character? We learn a lot about him both physically and emotionally. He had little that "sounded" comforting to him as a boy and hence we can infer that there was little comfort of any type. We know he grew up in a tenement. He tried to escape through drawing and sketching. We know he isn't satisfied with his present life but thinks he should be because he managed to put the tenement life behind him.

We learn about him physically. He's fifty-five. But this isn't presented merely as a fact. It's important because he feels that he's getting on and has pretty much wasted his life. And he blames himself.

We know he's stocky, well-built, his body hard like a boxer's, all because he likes to walk and run. He does it for enjoyment, not to keep in shape. So there is a reason here too for presenting his physical traits. We learn how he's dressed, not as straightforward description, but for a reason. It helps to reveal a facet of his personality.

Overall this passage helps create a mood that could perhaps be described as nostalgic, with a pervading bit of sadness.

An excellent descriptive passage is the one presented earlier in the chapter as an example of a good hook. Again, it's from "The Cup." To take the passage further:

> It was a winter sewn with the thread of pain,
> sewn to a tattered autumn at one end and to an as
> yet unshrunk spring on the other—a winter which
> lingered too long, so that the gray of the clouds cast
> musty shadows on everyone's spirit.
>
> That winter created David in its own image—in
> the image of shunned loneliness. Like stale snow
> which took too long to melt, David urgently longed
> for the next season of life. Unfortunately, that year
> spring dallied.
>
> David lived life adolescently alone, suspended like
> a morning star between nighttime and daytime,
> between parents and peers, between the
> wishfulness of childhood and the wishfulness of
> adulthood.

Through the description a definite mood is created, and the reader or listener should care immediately about David and begin to empathize with him, although little yet is known about him, only that he is an adolescent.

Seven

Narration and Point of View

You may recall the period in school called "show and tell," where you brought in an object of some sort and talked to the rest of the class about it. That is exactly what a good storyteller should do. Writers are often cautioned to "show" rather than to "tell." This is because those who have little experience writing fiction tend to tell everything, rather than showing it. But there must be a balance between the showing, which is the scenes that stretch forward, the action scenes, and the telling, the narration that "talks about," rather than actually presenting a scene.

The most successful story is a careful blending of active scenes and narration. It would be tedious to write or tell a story that included only action because it would have to include much that was unnecessary to the plot.

Definition of Narration

Narration is a kind of shorthand that quickly gets the protagonist from one point to another or allows him or her to remember a scene, rather than present it. It also includes description of both place and character. It covers in a short time events that may be important to the development of the story but are not worth a great amount of space. It condenses rather than bogs us down in detail.

In this respect narration often can be used as transitions from one point of action to another. It would be boring to see the character in a story perform every action a real-life counterpoint would perform. So narration used as transition often implies rather than actually presents certain actions. When a character in a story leaves her car and goes into her house, we assume that she also did such things as shutting and locking the car, crossing the street, walking up the steps, unlocking the door, withdrawing the key from the lock, entering and closing the door behind her.

But in a sense, the listener and the teller have a contract with each other. The teller agrees to present a believable story, while the listener agrees to suspend any disbelief. Each side has to work at this. The storyteller can condense events and not waste time with unimportant details, and the listener agrees to assume certain things.

Narration bridges time and events and keeps the story moving. Often storytellers or writers will say things like: "The next morning, Bill was late to work..." There is no reason to detail everything that happened from the previous day to the morning. The storyteller may then go on to say something like: "He knew he'd be in trouble with the boss, but he'd lain awake half the night worrying about Ellen's appointment with that old classmate of hers."

Two things have been accomplished. First, there was a smooth transition from one "stretching forward" to another. Second, there was a sort of recap of any important events that weren't actually covered during the "showing" scenes.

Narration is employed, as well, to describe. Look back at the description of Dennis in the last chapter, and you'll see an interweaving of both action and narration. You also will see a description of the setting for the story woven into the forward progression. In some places, it actually is difficult to separate action from narration. Dennis is walking along seeing certain places, but also thinking and remembering previous things about them. But the reader doesn't need to see all these places in the way that Dennis has seen them. Nor does the reader need to travel back to the tenement where Dennis grew up and actually see it. The suggestion is enough.

Narration helps create mood. In the following paragraph from my story "Mutant," a humorous post-holocaust piece, there is a mood of suspense created immediately:

> The car began to grumble and dip, and Pierre felt a jolt of fear. He was passing through the jungle, the forbidden place. The place where grotesque mutants lived. A green tangle of choking vines and undergrowth.

Even the choice of words, such as "green tangle" and "choking" contribute to the feeling that Pierre may be trapped and held. The deliberately choppy sentences and sentence fragments indicate tension.

The second paragraph, below, is a blending of action and narration. The first sentence, for instance, tells us that Pierre now hates and in the past has hated the drive home alone. The second sentence is part of the ongoing action because he now is observing the moon.

The third sentence is part of the ongoing action, but then the sentence refers to the past, what the legends have said. This is important to creating suspense but not important enough to present a flashback scene to show exactly how this legend came about. In other words, it's a shortcut.

> Pierre hated the drive home alone at night, and this night was worst of all. The full moon showed pale yellow, beyond the smoky clouds. It was a time of insanity, when sleeping beasts began to stir. Or so the legends said. It was a time when hideous mutants rose to stalk the night. The car coughed and slowed.

Narration can be used to transport the listener or the reader into the past, either in the protagonist's memory, as when Dennis thought of the tenement house, or in an actual flashback.

The following is actually a combination of memory and flashback. The "memory" part is used as a transition to take the reader back years before. I've boldfaced the memory part and italicized the flashback. You'll notice that one part is both boldfaced and italicized because it's a hazy area that could be considered either memory of flashback. This picks up Dennis' story a little later than what you read in the last chapter. He has decided that he has to commit himself fully to his art. He talks to a friend at a gallery to see if he can have an exhibit. The friend turns him down:

> How could he go home now? He'd feel ashamed. **He often had that feeling, like everything was his fault, and yet it was shameful to admit it. He supposed the feeling had started years before.**

After being passed among different relatives every few months, when he was thirteen, he went to stay with his Aunt Mattie. She discovered some of his drawings stuck under his side of the mattress on a single bed he shared with his cousin Max, two years younger.

He came home from school one day, and Aunt Mattie had them at the table. Three drawings. He'd progressed from his knights. One was flowers in a vase. He'd drawn it at school, looking at long dead mums on top of the bookcase by the window. He'd given them life again. Another showed a bowl of fruit, a couple of oranges, an apple, a bunch of grapes. That came from his imagination. There was never money for all kinds of fruit. And if there were, it wouldn't last long enough to go into a bowl.

The third one showed the old man who lived next door. Mr. Chambers. Ancient, wizened. Dennis had just learned that word from a fairy tale. The drawing showed him bent over the trash bin at the side of the building, rooting around with the stick he called his cane. It was a sad picture; the old man not wanting anyone to see him. Proud, yet needing anything he could dig out and hock.

"My God, Dennis," Aunt Mattie had said. "My God, where did you learn to draw like this? How did you ever capture a man on paper this way? At your age, how could you understand?" Her voice sounded hoarse, her face was red. She must be terribly angry, he thought.

He stared at the tips of his high-topped sneakers, the white part nearly worn away. "I'm...I'm sorry," he said.

"Dennis! Dennis! Look at me." He was afraid of what she would do. He looked up then and saw the tears in her eyes. "It's beautiful, honey. They're all beautiful."

The rule to remember is that if the entire scene is important to the "stretching forward," show it; if not, tell it.

Point of View

A story generally is shown and told from only one point of view or perspective. There are various point-of-view styles, all of which have advantages and disadvantages.

In deciding on your viewpoint of character, you have to keep in mind that the character's personality will color the perspective with which he or she views the world.

You can use an omniscient point of view, although this is probably the most difficult to make convincing. It means telling your story from an all-knowing perspective that can see into the minds of each character.

Since the omniscient point of view is all-seeing, it can switch from one character to another, with the advantage being that the situation can be perceived from all sides.

Yet, there are many disadvantages. Often, it's hard for the audience to follow the changes from seeing through one person's eyes to seeing through another's. Most often audience members will identify with a particular character, the protagonist. If the point of view switches to someone else, it may have the effect of snapping the listener out of the story.

Besides seeing into everyone's mind, the omniscient point of view allows the storyteller or author to make comments. This was a popular method during the nineteenth century, where writers often moralized: "Alas, poor Rebecca hath given her heart to a scoundrel, a scoundrel indeed as you, gentle reader, are about to discover."

This type of viewpoint is rarely used today because it comes across as "hokey" and totally insincere. It's what now is called "author intrusion." At a workshop I attend, I recently heard a story in which the author/reader went on in great detail in describing the land and its condition. He then read something like: "Two men came into sight at the top of the hill." During a critique the first question he received was: Whose sight were you writing about? No other characters had appeared in the story, and in contemporary times we expect a viewpoint character. The same writer fell into another trap of using flowery language, extremely proper grammar and exact but unusual words to label articles of clothing when his two characters were rough, uneducated frontiersmen.

It is difficult to make a story seem realistic or believable using the omniscient point of view because in everyday life, we view the world only from one perspective, our own. As the workshop writer/reader found, his word choice and "godlike" point of view distracted from the action, merely calling attention to the unusualness of his treatment.

Another point of view is that of the observer/narrator, who is not an integral part of the story but merely an observer. The advantage is that this "character" can be more objective about what is occurring than can the protagonist or the antagonist. On the other hand, this point of view distances the audience from the story.

A audience already is once removed because, despite empathizing with the characters and the situation, the audience member is not actually a part of it. Even the attempts lately at "roleplaying fiction," where the reader becomes a character, are not totally successful because at any time you can stop reading. But with a narrator/observer, we are asked to view the protagonist not with our own eyes but someone else's. And since this narrator does stand apart, the audience is unable to "experience" or "feel" the emotions of the protagonist.

Yet this sort of story can work, as you saw with "Tonight My Sister Danced Freedom." Another one of my stories, "Fitting the Mold," also is told from the viewpoint of an observer. The purpose is to show in a sympathetic light a character who could not recognize that it was his own fault for messing up his relationships with others because he expected everyone to fit a particular mold. The story would have meant little from his point of view because he would have failed to recognize what he was doing. He became much more sympathetic seen through the eyes of someone who was almost an outsider to his life.

In this excerpt, Pete, the narrator, is talking with Zach's son, age nineteen, in a completely separate part of the house. Kevin, the son, asks Pete if he met Zach when Pete lived in Manhattan.

> "No, actually, I met him later," I said.
> "Oh, well, it's none of my business.
> Unfortunately, nothing seems to be my business
> where he's concerned." He shook his head and put
> the box down on the shelf underneath the
> aquarium. "I didn't mean that the way it sounds. I
> didn't mean any offense."
> "None was taken," I said.
> "Dad'll be surprised that we met. I try to stay out
> of his way. Sometimes, I wish things were different.
> I mean Dad's a really nice guy if he wants to be. But
> we always seem to start out wrong."

"I'm sorry, Kevin. I don't know what to say."

"Hey," he said, "it's not your problem."

I smiled. "Thanks for letting me see the fish."

"Any time."

I touched his shoulder, turned and left. He closed the door gently behind me as I walked on out to the kitchen.

Zach was cutting a tomato for salad. "Did I hear you talking to someone?" he asked.

"I just met Kevin."

"What?" He turned, surprised.

"His door was open. He saw me looking at his aquarium and invited me in."

"Quite an honor. He hasn't invited me in since God knows when."

"Kevin acknowledged that you aren't on the best of terms."

"I'll bet he said it was all my fault."

"He didn't say much of anything."

"Yeah. No matter what, they all blame me." Zach laid down his knife. "Ever see *The Lion in Winter*?" he asked. "First act curtain? Henry brooding about losing his boys. All of them gone."

I nodded.

He picked up the salad bowl. "To my way of thinking," he said, "old Hank was a jerk."

This is the way the story ends, showing Zach's refusal or inability to look at people as individuals. This, of course, could not be shown from his point of view.

There is also the device of telling a story from a variety of viewpoints but with each character having only a section or a scene and making a definite break of some sort before going into another character's head. This is relatively unusual for stories to be told;

you are much more likely to encounter it in novels where chapters alternate viewpoints.

Even so, that's what I did with "Mutant," switching the point of view back and forth throughout.

> A clanging began and the car spit fitfully. Pierre's knuckles formed bands around the steering wheel. His jaw ached from tension. He started rocking back and forth, as if the motion would somehow propel the car forward. But with one last gasp the motor died.

> Milt Johnson opened his eyes and stretched. He sighed deeply and sat up. Now the change would begin. The change to power. The feelings of strength, almost sexual and entirely satisfying. He held his hands out in front of him and saw them sprout with hair. The fingernails narrowed, hardened into claws. Pads began to form on his palms and fingers.

> He felt himself grow as blood surged within him. He tore off his clothes, and watched the stiff bristles form on his legs and arms. He began to sniff the powerful odors around him. Odors of must and decay, mixed with animal smells. It was good to be alive. He threw back his head and howled at the moon.

> The worst had happened, and Pierre had to accept it. The decision made, his breath came easier. He checked his gun and undid the latch on the door.

In this story there really is no antagonist, no villain. Rather, both men have deformities, which become apparent later in the story, due to radiation poisoning. Telling it from both points of view allows the audience to sympathize with both, caught up in something beyond their control.

The most common point of view is that of the protagonist. Everything is seen, heard, felt, and *judged* by him. The aim, of course, is audience identification. Once the viewpoint is switched to someone else, reader identification is broken.

In "Mutant" I wanted the thoughts of each of my protagonists blocked from the other. But generally such a device is not good because it snaps the audience out of the story and takes at best a little time to become comfortable "inside" another character's head.

If you do not have to shift from one character to another, don't.

The last consideration is whether to tell the story from first or third person point of view. Unless you're telling a story in which you are asking the audience to "imagine" they actually are involved, you probably would never use second-person point of view. If you do, the tendency on the part of the listener is to argue with you throughout that they themselves did not perform the action you say they did. For instance:

> You stand and shake hands. "Did you bring your trumpet with you?" Rev. Sherwood asks.
> "I can get it," you tell him.
> "Do you have the music?"
> "Yes, but I haven't had a chance to go over it."
> "That's okay. I'll meet you at the church." You both start toward the front door. "I'll leave the side entrance open. Do you know where that is?"
> "Yes."
> Rev. Sherwood nods. "I'll see you in a few minutes." You and he step out onto the front porch. Rev. Sherwood turns as he starts down the step. "You don't mind doing this, do you?"
> You are startled. People usually don't ask your opinion.

And, incidentally, a second-person story almost always is told in present tense, which in itself is somewhat jarring.

It doesn't matter a great deal whether a story is told from first or third person. Do whatever is most comfortable and seems most appropriate.

The biggest advantage of the first-person point of view is that it can sound more intimate. That is, the audience is not quite so distanced. If you empathize with the "first person" from whose perspective the story is told, you feel closer to the character.

There are, however, disadvantages. It comes across as unnatural or maybe egotistical for a first-person character to describe self accurately, so the storyteller has to resort to tricks or devices to show what the character looks like. It's impossible for a person to be objective about self or to see self as others see him or her.

Along the same lines, a first person character cannot show emotion through facial expression, because the person can't see self and describe how he or she looks.

With third-person point of view, you can describe more objectively, but you are talking about an "other," which distances the listener from the character. Third-person point of view is also somewhat schizoid because the narrator/third-person character are the same and yet they aren't. They are the same because the listener can see inside the character's head. They aren't because the narrator can be more objective in describing the character's outward appearance and reactions.

Often stories are told from first-person point of view in order to establish an intimacy with the audience and have them identify more closely with the teller. The most important consideration for narration and point of view, however, is to choose what makes you the most comfortable.

Eight

Theme and Organization

When you want to tell a story, you have usually already decided why and know the occasion. But even if you do know your purpose in telling the story, you still need to determine the theme or central idea, which has to support or fit the purpose.

In many stories you've heard or read, it's easy to figure out this theme. In others, it's more difficult. Conceivably, one person may get something different out of a story than will another person. You have to figure out how you would like the audience to feel afterward, and why you want them to feel this way.

Maybe you want only to call attention to something you think is worth remembering. That was the purpose in a number of stories I wrote about my childhood. I wanted people to reexamine their own pasts and remember the magic, the sense of wonder, the newness of growing up. In the way of illustration, here is an excerpt from one of those stories, called "Going Fishing."

The best times were when Grandpa took him fishing. The day before they'd dig up some worms in the garden and put them in a tin can filled with dirt. The next morning when it was still dark, they'd get up real early. Grandma would fix them a lunch in a paper sack, and they'd get their poles and go out to the car.

They'd drive for a long ways till they got to the Lincoln Highway. They'd follow it the whole way to Bedford County. Then they'd turn off and go back another road and after awhile pull off to the side.

They'd get out of the car and walk through a field into the woods and then down a bank. And there was Yellow Creek. Except it wasn't a creek like the one on Grandpa O'Jenkins' farm. It was much too big for that. You couldn't walk across it like you could the creek on Grandpa's farm. It was more like a river.

Martin liked to climb up on the cliff and dangle his line way down in the water. He'd sit there for a long time and then get a bite. Grandpa sat beside him with his own line in the water and another line nearby.

The story is about the relationship between the boy and his grandpa, much like the relationships many of us had with a relative.

Another type of story examines social problems. This would be the type of thing dealt with in "Look How Things are Changing," a story about racial prejudice and how a white man at the turn of a century went to the aid of a little black boy who was run over by an ice wagon.

An example of another type of story would be one with a theme that explores contemporary values—for example, the question of peer pressure versus family background.

Themes usually are based on common premises, ideas the audience already accepts. For example: You should love your neighbor; everyone wants financial security; war is wrong.

The theme should be something important to the audience, something about which they can feel a strong emotion, and something with which they agree. Yet the story must be more than a statement of the theme, or it would come across like a message preached from a soap box.

In many cases, particularly if you are presenting a story with serious intent, the listeners should empathize with the characters and ideas. In a humorous story, there may not be the degree of empathy because humor is more "intellectual" than emotional. That means listeners can stand back further from the characters and the situation. It's easier to laugh at people and situations in humorous stories because we don't identify so strongly with them.

Where can these themes originate? One place is your past, which is both unique and yet similar to others' pasts. Use the uniqueness to maintain interest, the similarity to build a common ground. No human being is totally alien to any other human being. We all experience the feelings of anger, love, hatred, disgust, and fear. We've all been in similar situations. We've been ill or in pain. We've experienced loss and rejoiced with others over their good fortune.

Listeners relate the stories they hear to their own backgrounds and personalities. Yet the chain of events that makes up your perceptions of the world and your interpretation of events are different from anyone else's views of the same things.

In one of the stories in *Welcome to the Monkey House*, Kurt Vonnegut, Jr., writes about a society in which there are attempts to make everyone equal by handicapping those individuals who had outstanding abilities or attributes in any one area. The handsome and beautiful are masked, and the intelligent have their thoughts interrupted electronically. The physically strong have to carry added weight, and the television announcers have speech problems. The idea of such a society appears ridiculous to us. We need a sense of personal identity. We want to be recognized for our outstanding qualities, while on the other hand, we don't want to stand out because of any defect. No matter what the basis for consideration, none of us is exactly like any other. It is these differences that provide interest for the audience.

Our Basic Needs

Central ideas often come from a reexamination or rethinking of our basic needs, those things that are necessary to sustain a reasonably happy life. Examine how they are stifled in everyday life, and you have the basis for any number of stories.

Basic needs include: security, recognition, response, adventure, worship and self-preservation. Let's take the first of these. What types of security do we need? First, we need physical security. We want to feel secure in knowing that if we step outside we won't be mugged. We want financial security. We need money for food, clothing, and shelter. We want to feel comfortable in social situations and the security of good health. The list is very long, and you can probably begin to see how any one of these things could be the basis for a story.

There are many examples of themes based on the need for security. One is my story, "Charity," where the family's source of income is taken away when the father's legs are crushed in a mining accident.

One of the other needs is for recognition, which can take many forms. A person wants status, which can range from recognition of musical ability to success in business.

Consider the following excerpt from "A Beautiful Man" by Cathryn Alpert:

> My girlfriend, Neela, says she can't love Roger, even though he is the kindest man she has ever known, because he is not beautiful. What she wants more than anything in the world, she says, is to have a beautiful man.
>
> When I suggest that perhaps this ideal of hers is keeping her from finding true happiness, Neela says she knows it's stupid and illogical, but she can't help herself. Roger, she says, just doesn't do it for her, and after three and a half years of steady commitment, she's beginning to feel cheated.
>
> "Roger's not so bad," I try to console her. "He's a little thin, but he has sensitive eyes and a warm smile."
>
> "Roger's a baboon," she counters.

Neela wants status; she wants it known that she's the kind of woman who can attract a "beautiful" man.

You can take adages as the basis for your stories. "The grass is always greener on the other side of the fence." "Love conquers all." "What you sow, so shall you reap." "A penny saved is a penny earned."

This children's story, for instance, illustrates in a gentle way that "You should not try to be something you aren't."

CHRISTOPHER PUPPY

by Marsh Cassady

One sunny morning Christopher leaped out of bed. He put on his clothes and ran downstairs.

"Good morning, Christopher," said Mother.

"Bow wow," said Christopher. "I am a puppy."

Mother set a plate on the kitchen table.

"Puppies have fun," said Christopher.

"All right," laughed Mother. "Sit down now. Breakfast will soon be ready."

Christopher got down on his hands and knees.

"Bow wow," he barked. "Bow wow."

"Oh, I see," said Mother. She set a dog biscuit in front of Christopher.

"Grrr," he said. "G-r-r-r."

"What's the matter?" asked Mother. "Don't you like your breakfast?"

"G-r-r-r," said Christopher. He crawled out the door.

Ginger the cat sat on a stone washing her whiskers.

"Bow wow," said Christopher. "Bow wow."

Ginger looked at Christopher. "Purr," she said. "Purr."

"You be afraid of me!" he shouted.

"Purr," said Ginger.

Christopher crawled to the big field behind the house.

The tall grass tickled his nose. He jumped at a grasshopper. "Bow wow," he said. "Bow wow."

The grasshopper flew away.

"Oh," thought Christopher, "a puppy can catch anything."

Christopher tried and tried to catch some bugs. He could not. He crawled home.

"Hello, puppy," said Mother. She patted his head.

"Ummm. Ummm," went Christopher.

"What's the matter, puppy?" asked Mother. "Are you hungry?"

"Bow wow," said Christopher.

"All right," said Mother. "Sit down at the table."

"G-r-r-r," said Christopher. He crawled into the living room and jumped onto Daddy's big chair.

"No, Christopher," said Mother, "puppies cannot sit on the furniture."

Christopher jumped down. He sat in a corner.

"Well," he thought, "puppies don't have so much fun."

"Here, Christopher," Mother called. "Your breakfast is ready."

Christopher crawled into the kitchen. "Bow wow wow!" he said. "Bow wow wow."

"I found a nice bone for you," said Mother.

Christopher stood up. "Oh, Mommy, I am not a puppy," he said. "I am a boy."

Mother smiled. "I know," she said. "That is why I fixed you some pancakes."

One way to look at storytelling is as an interpretation of life. Through your stories you can make statements, call attention to things you think are important, or make people aware of things you think they may have failed to see.

Through selectivity you, the storyteller, place importance on things you consider to be important. Your ideas and major concerns may be different from others', so you ignore or deemphasize these other concerns. But that's okay. It's what people do in all facets of life. If everyone were interested in the same things and held exactly the same beliefs, it would be a pretty dull world.

Types of Organization

As you learned, the most common type of organization is the story that has a plot. But there are other types as well, sometimes determined in large part by the purpose.

Often you have a story that follows a chronological pattern like the story with a plot. Yet it does not include an inciting incident, rising action, and so on. One type of story that often falls into this category is the parable, which may have a plot, but often doesn't.

It is common for speakers to include parables as part of a longer speech. People find it easier to remember and even to take more seriously a story rather than a simple recitation of beliefs or facts. Parables often are extended analogies, which may be entertaining and purposeful. If you do use parables, you have to make certain that the intent is clear and the analogy does not get muddied.

An excellent source for parables is *Balloons! Candy! Toys!*, by Daryl Olszewski. It begins:

"Balloons! Candy! Toys!" the man called out as he pushed his brightly painted cart down the street one hot summer day. A little boy heard the man's cry and rushed outside to see what it could be.

As the story continues, the boy follows the man until one day the man is gone. The boy then takes over the task of giving balloons, candy, and toys to the children along the streets.

As Olszewski says, it is important to keep parables simple and straightforward. Because their purpose is to illustrate a particular point in an interesting way, they do not need a great deal of elaboration or character development. Rather, the idea or theme is the most important element.

Another type of story is the one developed around a character. The goal of such a story is to have the audience learn to care deeply for the person.

A good example of this is a book published several years ago called *The Beans of Egypt Maine*, written by Carolyn Chute. The story progresses yet does not follow a plot.

Another type of story is one which is simply a "slice of life." That is, it exists largely to call the listener's attention to a time or place or circumstances. In one of my stories, "The Wooden Horse and the Drum," an eight-year-old boy is with his parents at a magic show in Johnstown, Pennsylvania, in the mid-forties. Outside the theatre, there is a great deal of noise that continues to build in intensity:

> The magician was going to cut off someone's head. Instead, he came to the front of the stage and held up his hands for the audience to be quiet. "If you don't mind, I'll end the show right here." There were groans and protests.

"It seems inappropriate to continue," he said, "in light of what has just happened." His voice broke and he paused. "Ladies and gentlemen," he said, "Japan has surrendered. The war is over."

For a moment there was silence. Then the audience started to cheer. The magician stood still, tears running down each cheek. The woman beside Martin's mom began to sob. "Thank God," she said. "Thank God."

"Our National Anthem," the magician said. The voices were strong, the words bouncing off the walls and filling the theatre with sound.

The men and women were smiling; some had tears on their faces. The cheering began once more.

The lights came on, and the show was over. Outside, it seemed, the world had gone crazy. Car horns honked and the streets were filled with people. From windows of office buildings people filled the air with confetti and streamers. Martin wondered where they'd gotten them.

Strangers hugged and pounded each other's backs. A long streamer, a pale blue color, floated through the air and landed on Martin's shoulder.

"Don't throw it away," his father said. "Someday it will mean a lot." Martin wound it up and stuck it in his pocket.

They walked to the parking lot, off from the main part of town. Here the streets were quieter. Once inside the car Martin's mother sighed. "It's finally ended," she said. "The war is over."

"It was the bombs," his dad answered. "After they dropped the atom bombs, Japan had no choice but surrender. It was the beginning of the end." He turned to Martin. "Remember this night," he said. "It's important that you remember, that everyone remember."

At home as carefully as he could, Martin pulled the streamer out of his pocket and put it into the wooden box on his desk. Dad had made the box when Martin was very small, and he kept all his treasures there. His Captain Marvel pin and Tom Mix badge. His special stones. His steelies and rarest marbles. He closed the lid and climbed into bed. He thought of his cousin Steve. He'd been in the Army, the infantry. Once he'd let Martin try on his Army hat. Maybe he'd soon be home. Then Martin thought of his other cousin, Perry. He'd never come home again.

As all these things went through Martin's mind, he felt his eyes grow heavy. Before he fell asleep he thought of the magic show and each of the tricks. The one he liked best was the wooden horse that galloped through the air.

A less-usual type of organization is **spatial**—that is, organized in space, north to south, top to bottom, and so on. As are some of the other types that do not follow a plot, this kind of story is almost always episodic, with little relationship between one event and another, except for continuing characters or different characters performing similar actions. The theme for such a story, for instance, might be that everyone is the same, no matter where they live.

Choose the type of organization that best suits your purposes in telling your story.

Nine

Planning the Presentation

In planning your story, you need to analyze your audience. It helps to know everything you can about them beforehand so you'll have a good idea of your approach.

You might want to consider age. You probably would want to present a different kind of story for five- or six-year-olds than you would for those in their fifties and sixties. Are the audience members all males, all females or a mixture? This could influence your presentation.

Other considerations that might be important are: educational and socioeconomic backgrounds, area of the country or world, and so on. Anything you can determine about the audience ahead of time could be of help in both your approach and choice of story.

Setting the Mood

For a night of Indian stories, the participants dressed in their tribal garb and sat by a simulated fire. A friend of mine in Ohio used to tell stories about the pioneer days. She traveled to various elementary schools wearing an eighteenth-century dress and carrying with her old tools that no longer are used.

How far should you go in setting the tone and the mood for your story or stories? The question has no simple answer. Anything that adds to, rather than detracts from the story can help, but only if you feel comfortable with it.

You want to get your listener into the proper frame of mind, so use whatever accoutrements you think may be helpful. I have another friend who goes to schools dressed as a witch every Halloween. An artist, she goes so far as to paint her fingernails with black cats or brooms. She loves telling scary stories and is always well received.

Even if your story is part of a longer presentation, you may want to alter the setting at the proper time. You may dim the lights, or bring out props that suggest perhaps a feeling or a place.

Yet none of these things will help if you are ill-prepared or don't really want to communicate with your listeners. You need to believe in the importance of what you are doing, whatever its purpose. Unless you're a pretty good actor, a listener more than likely will be able to detect anything phony about your presentation.

There is little point in getting into a storytelling situation you'd rather avoid. But in all likelihood you will want to communicate and you will enjoy what you're doing. And almost assuredly, if you enjoy it, your listeners will.

It is very important to remember that never should you talk down to or patronize your listener. I've heard people do this many times, both in talks and telling stories. They treat their listeners as if they're dumb or at least not on an intellectual par with the storyteller. Unfortunately, this is a common occurrence when adults communicate with children.

Approaches

Basically, there are two approaches to storytelling: the performance-oriented and the literary, although any presentation may have elements of both.

The first is the one I usually prefer, though it is simply a matter of choice. This approach involves roleplaying or in a sense becoming the characters. When there is a big contrast among characters, the storyteller can change voice, stance, and so on to more clearly indicate who is speaking. This is akin to acting, although there are a number of differences. The most apparent, probably, is that the storyteller has more direct contact with an audience than does the actor. The major difference can be summed up by saying: A play is a portrayal of events, places, and people, and storytelling is a suggestion of these three things.

Using the performance-oriented approach, you put yourself in the place of the characters, reacting as they do to the situation. If a character is happy, your voice might sound bubbly. If the character is sad, you may frown.

This is where some of the preparation for the presentation comes in. Experiment with different ways of telling the story, so you can see what works best for you and for your material.

The other approach is more objective. The storyteller, in effect, stands back from the story and does not become so personally involved with the characters and events.

There are advantages and disadvantages to both approaches. The first might be more dynamic and involving, but the second could allow the listener greater use of his or her imagination in the interpretation.

Memory or Manuscript?

Some people feel that the only honest approach to presenting a story is to retell it—that is, to know the plot, the characters and the situations well enough to be able to tell them to someone, much as you would tell a long joke.

There is an advantage in that this method can seem more spontaneous, though if you don't know the story as well as you think, it could lead to losing the thread. Of course, you can use notes that include key words or a plot outline, but this probably is more distracting than using a complete manuscript from which you read.

Some people prefer to memorize the story. Using this method, you can be sure you don't stray from the original plot. Memorization and roleplaying seem to go together best, but if you are unsure of yourself, you may risk forgetting the exact words.

The final approach is to use a written story. This way you can be certain of not forgetting. On the other hand, the manuscript sets up a kind of physical barrier between you and your listeners, much as a podium does. I have found that for myself, whether speaking or storytelling, I much prefer nothing to physically separate me from my listeners.

Certainly, there are times you would want to use a manuscript, for instance, if you were conducting a story hour at a library. Here, you might be presenting others' stories, and you would want to present them exactly.

Remember also that there is no such thing as practicing too much. I've heard people say that if you go over a story too often, it loses its spontaneity. Nonsense. If you don't practice, it will also make the material sound unprepared when you forget, lose your place, stumble over unfamiliar words or whatever. No musician or actor, except in improvisational situations, presents new material without practicing it.

If you choose a story, whether your own or someone else's, that you like and really have an interest and purpose in telling, you should not have to worry whether or not it sounds fresh and spontaneous.

Introductions

Whether you are simply telling a story or whether you are presenting it along with a talk, it is important to have an introduction. If the story is to illustrate a point in a speech, the introduction may be as simple as saying: "That brings to mind..."

But often introductions will not be that simple. One of the first things you want to do is gain the listeners' attention. Then you want to interest them in the story you are going to tell.

There's no standard length for an introduction; it may be long or involved or little more than telling the subject or title of the story.

You do need to remember that if you are telling the story without the accompaniment of a talk, it will take a few moments for the audience to be psychologically ready to listen. They need to adjust to your presence and to the situation. What do you do during this time?

You probably should not say anything extremely important to your presentation, because most of the audience will miss it. Use the time to prepare yourself, as well. That means simply pausing for a second or two without saying much of anything beyond perhaps a simple greeting.

As you learned in the last chapter, you need to set the mood or the tone for your story. Unless the listeners are gathered for a particular purpose known beforehand, they have no way of knowing the type of story you will tell them. Will it be humorous or serious? You have to let the listeners know, so they will be in the proper frame of mind.

How do you do this? A lot of it depends on how you conduct yourself. A humorous introduction would certainly convey the wrong impression if you were going to present a serious story. On the other hand, it can be funnier to present a deadly serious introduction that leads into humor.

As there is no set length for an introduction, there is no hard and fast rule about what it should accomplish. A lot depends on the situation. If you are telling a story written by someone else, you may want to explain how you found the story and why it is important to you. You may even include information about the author so the audience can better understand the writing. Maybe you need to tell about the historical period or geographic location in which the author lived and how it affected the person's writing.

The introduction should certainly suit the audience. As an example, suppose you were going to read or tell one of Jonathan Swift's stories, such as "A Voyage to Lilliput." Now it's regarded as a children's story; it wasn't at the time it was written. Suppose you were to introduce this story to a group of children. How would this differ from the introduction you would give the same story if you included it in a talk about English writers who used satire? The introduction depends to some extent on you and the type of person you are. You read earlier about reading versus retelling versus memorizing. You do not have these choices with the introduction. Since it serves the purpose of establishing a rapport between reader and listener, its delivery should be spontaneous rather than written and delivered formally. This isn't to say it shouldn't be fully prepared, only that it should be presented so that the audience feels you are speaking directly to them.

The following story could be used in any number of instances. Read through it and figure out the sort of introduction you would use if you were telling it to a group of your peers on Halloween. How would this differ from telling the same story to explain schizophrenia to a group of volunteers at a mental hospital?

SISTERS

by Marsh Cassady

Off the east coast of Scotland is the Bay of Eigg, which faces the Sound of Sleat in Inverness. Here Mother Nature plays tunes upon the sands of the beach. "It's caused by the crust atop the sand being disturbed," Henri, my husband, told me.

"Don't believe him," my sister Fidelia said. "It's the voice of Pythagorus. Can't you hear him call your name?"

Fidelia loved our land. Perhaps my husband loved it too. At least, he never wanted to return to his native France. He and I lived here together, along with Fidelia.

Because we are identical twins, there is a link between Fidelia and me that exists between no other individuals. Yet I always objected to being blamed for things she did. All my life this was so. But when I protested, Mother looked at me askance, as though I were lying.

"I am the good twin," I always said, "Fidelia the evil one." Still I loved her.

Fidelia was clairvoyant, able to see and hear discarnate spirits and to gain knowledge by touching objects belonging to others. Often she would tell me something about Henri she could have known only were he or I to tell her. Yet neither had done so.

It was unlawful for Christians to dabble in the occult. This was just as well. I wanted to stay away from such things, but not Fidelia.

At times I could hear her chanting in her bedroom. "*In nomine Dei nostri Satanas Luciferi excelei*," she prayed. "In the name of Satan, Ruler of the Earth, King of the World, I command the forces of darkness to bestow their infernal powers upon

101

me. Open wide the Gates of Hell. Come forth to greet me from the abyss as your Sister and Friend!"

At times like this her very soul seemed to leave her body. I tried to exercise my will against her. I prayed to God until drops of sweat beaded my brow.

Still I could do nothing. Her dalliance with the occult left me as a fruit from which all the juice has been sucked.

I was grateful I lacked Fidelia's powers, yet she invariably gloated over my futile efforts to understand them. I was intensely fearful of the unknown quality she represented. There was much more to Fidelia than the ability to transmit thought. Much more.

One night I was seated at my loom. Outside all was still. Suddenly I realized something evil was soon to happen.

The scene outside my window shifted. Trees and bushes changed to tenuous shadow, and the earth seemed to open before my eyes.

Suddenly, someone tapped me on the shoulder. Yet no one was there. Something brushed across my cheek. Mingled voices called me names and threatened to steal the memories from my mind. Then the voices tried to persuade me to poison Henri.

Abruptly, the terror ended. Yet later in bed someone slapped me again and again. I showed my bruise marks to Henri; he pretended not to see them. He said he was leaving for London. Yet later I heard his voice, talking with someone else, planning how they were going to kill me.

I rushed to the house of a neighbor. There I heard Henri's voice outside the window. "We'll drag her to the loch," he said. "We'll drown her and say that she killed herself."

I ran from the house, stumbling and falling on sharp bits of stone.

In the mirror back home I glimpsed my reflection. It was a corridor of veils. Behind me stood Fidelia.

She laughed. "I shall have to kill Henri," she said, "for he's placed you under a spell. I shall have to kill him before he kills you."

"I have a sickness nigh unto death, Fidelia." I said. "It is called despair."

"Will you grant me the right to remove the spell?" she asked.

"I leave it entirely up to you," I replied. Fidelia passed her hands over my body. I slept better that night than I had in months.

The next morning on arising, I caught a glimpse of Fidelia struggling with a huge scimitar Henri had brought back from a trip to Turkey. I did not ask what she planned to do. I did not want to find out.

The scimitar had been in a room in which Henri kept souvenirs of battle, mementos from his childhood in France and heirlooms. I seldom entered that room.

Later I wondered what it was that sometimes kept him enthralled there for hours. The door to the room appeared stuck. I pushed it open further. Above the door I saw the scimitar start to fall.

A moment later it cut off my screams. And my head.

Just before I died, I realized I would finally be rejoining my twin sister, Fidelia. She had, I now remembered, died when we were born.

Repetition

Another consideration in choosing a story to tell is the sound itself. Unless you are especially good at tongue twisters, it's best not to choose any story that has anything in it like "Sister Susie sitting on a thistle."

Children like repeated sounds, in much the way Jean Seley used them in her story about Lucretia Matilda Penelope Snort and her booglie wooglie wagon. Not only do the words have a good rhythm, but they are repeated in their entirety, when, of course, the listener would know Lucretia without all of her names and the wagon without all of its names.

Repetition serves several purposes. It emphasizes. If a sound or series of sounds is repeated over and over, a good assumption is that they are important. Similarly, a listener is more apt to remember the repeated phrase or name.

Especially for children, repetition provides a kind of security and comfort. In a larger sense, this is why they like to hear the same bedtime story over and over again.

Discussion

The last consideration in preparing your presentation is to decide whether or not to have a discussion afterward. If you do, you should avoid moralizing about the story, and you should avoid trying to explain just what you intended. If this isn't apparent from your introduction and the story, you've failed in your attempt, and there's no use belaboring it. But a more likely scenario is that you perform overkill by stating and then restating, rather than letting the listeners figure things out for themselves. By pointing out and explaining after the story is finished, you are implying either that you failed or that the audience is too dense to understand.

A discussion is probably best handled with you serving only as the facilitator. In that role you help to get things started by asking the audience what they discovered, what the story meant to them, if they agree with what the characters did, and so on. You keep the discussion from getting bogged down or from being dominated by one person or one viewpoint, and you draw together what has been said by the listeners, not what you concluded.

Ten

Analyzing Your Story

Whether or not you are telling your own story or one written by someone else, you need to analyze it in detail so you can best convey its meaning to an audience. This includes knowing the high points and what to emphasize, as well as making the dialogue clear.

You may think it odd that there is a need to analyze your own story. After all, you wrote it and should know what it means. In part, that's true. But there is a quote by theatre director Tyrone Guthrie about playwrights that could apply as well to all writers. He said that he believes the last person to be consulted about a script is the playwright. "If the author is a wise man, he will admit straight away that he does not know what it is about.... The more important the work of art, the less the author will know what he has written" (Tyrone Guthrie, transcript of a talk delivered before the Royal Society of Arts, London, March 10, 1952. From Toby Cole and Helen K. Chinoy, eds. *Direc-*

tors on Directing. Rev. ed. [Indianapolis: The Bobbs-Merrill Company, Inc., 1963], 214).

In part, I agree with this. Writing or developing a story is to a large degree instinctive. With my own stories used as examples in this book, I've had to go through and figure out exactly what I was saying and how I was saying it.

You may have a "gut" feeling about the work and know that it is effective, but you haven't quite pinned down the reasons. The same, of course, is true when hearing or reading the work of others. Everyone has had the experience of feeling cold chills up and down the spine at the end of a story. In many cases this is the experience of the right brain, while the more logical side may then say: Hey, wait a minute. This affected me a certain way, but why?

Many times when we hear a story or see a play, we can enjoy it without analysis. And this is fine. But in order to bring this sort of experience to an audience, someone, whether the writer or the theatre artists, had to analyze what the script was all about.

In the past I've directed a great number of plays. This requires a tremendous amount of planning to do the job correctly. In fact, I easily spend twice the number of hours on elements not connected with rehearsal. And a major percentage of these hours are spent on script analysis. Even the blocking, the stage business, and placement of characters is a result of this analysis: Who is the more important character in the scene? What bit of dialogue needs the most emphasis? How can the visual aspects of the production point them up?

Not only do I spend time myself in analyzing the show, but I have the actors do their own analysis and then spend an entire rehearsal discussing this analysis and making compromises. Why do I mention this? Because I cannot over-emphasize the importance of adequate preparation for presenting a written work to an audience.

Determining the Ideas

Another quote about plays that applies to all types of writing presented to listeners comes from stage and film director Jose Quintero, who says that the director's job (or applying this to storytelling, your job) "is to translate something from the literary form into an active dramatic life—to translate rather than to dictate or to inspire" (Jose Quintero, interviewed by Jean-Claude van Itallie, in Joseph F. McCrindle, ed., *Behind the Scenes: Theatre and Film Reviews from the Transatlantic Review* [New York: Holt, Rinehart and Winston, 1971], 256.

If you are using another writer's story, you need to figure out the central idea and any supplementary ideas to "translate" for the listener. What you decide depends on your interpretation. For example, in "Whose Woods These Are," you could justify the central idea as something like: "In order to be happy, you need to resolve your past."

This could be the case since we see throughout the story that Roy has never let go of what happened on his grandfather's farm, but has let it gnaw away at him, influencing his entire life. Granted, this influence was at least partly responsible for his having financial success, but was the price worth it, and would he have succeeded anyhow?

On the other hand, the central idea could be: "A highly motivated person will succeed in spite of his past." This can be justified by the fact that at the end of the story, the central character still plans to buy out the electronics firm, despite the fact that he no longer feels he has to be invincible.

Supporting ideas in "Whose Woods These Are" could be first that "Everyone needs love," even though the character Roy is highly independent. The story implies that he has no friends because of his single-mindedness. As a matter of fact, in the first few drafts of the story, I brought this out very clearly through showing his interactions with other people. Then I decided it would be more effective to imply rather than openly state it.

Another supporting idea could be simply the well-known fact that "no matter how we try to escape, our pasts go with us." Roy states that he went as far away as he could from Western Pennsylvania. Obviously, he wanted to escape.

Take the other stories presented in the book and try to come up with a central idea and supporting ideas for each. Then try to define a different central idea. Think then about how you would present the story differently using the different ideas.

Plot/Organization

You need to know how the story you'll tell is organized, so you can point this up for the listener. If the story has a plot, you need to determine where the inciting incident occurs, so the listener will not miss it. The inciting incident in "Christopher Puppy," for instance, is when Christopher decides he wants to be a dog instead of a human boy. This is where the conflict begins.

In any story you have to identify the protagonist and the antagonist. In this case, the antagonist is not Christopher's mother, though it might seem this way. Rather it can be called, perhaps, reality, which opposes the boy's being able actually to become a puppy.Even though the story is very short, the conflict builds through a series of complications. The first is that Christopher wants to be a puppy, but he doesn't want to accept all the conditions of puppyhood. He doesn't want to eat a dog biscuit. So he runs away from this complication, in a way ignoring it.

The next complications are his supposed confrontation with the cat, which ignores him, and his attempt to catch the grasshopper.

After his adventures outside, Christopher becomes hungry. Now the problem intensifies. He wants to be a puppy, he thinks. But apparently, he wants only the best (to him) aspects of puppyhood. He doesn't want to sit at the table, yet he wants to be able to sit on the living room chair.

The turning point, of course, is when Christopher jumps off the chair and sits in the corner. It's then that he decides "puppies don't have so much fun." Then there is a further complication that forces the issue: Christopher's mother offering him a bone for breakfast. The climax is when he says: "Oh, Mommy, I am not a puppy. I am a boy."

These can be thought of as plotlines, sentences, whether in dialogue form or in narrative, that are particularly important for a listener to hear and understand in order to follow the story. It can help to go over the story with a highlighting pen to indicate these lines.

In this story the first important line is, "Bow wow. I am a puppy." The next one is, "Puppies have fun." Of course, a large percentage of lines in this story are of particular importance since the story is so condensed. But try this with something longer, and see what you can come up with.

The falling action here is very brief. Still, it brings the tale to a satisfactory ending. It is that Mother already fixed him pancakes but didn't give them to him right away. Instead, she was letting him learn his own lessons, certainly because she loves him.

Once you have figured out all these elements of plot, then what? What do you do about them? In later chapters, you'll read about using the voice and body effectively in storytelling. So let it suffice here to say that you would point up these elements through voice usage and possibly body placement and movement.

Many stories are much longer than "Christopher Puppy," and the plot elements may be harder to discover. But when you discover them, you have a much better chance of having your storytelling come across well.

Characterization

In the chapter on character, you learned the importance of knowing your characters. Why is this important to telling a story? Obviously, whether you use the performance or objective approach, you will want to differentiate among the characters. The more clearly you understand them, the better you can delineate them for your listener.

Each of the major characters in a story has a goal. The goals of the protagonist and antagonist come into conflict. If you understand what the goals are, you have a better chance of presenting the struggle clearly for the listener. The goals do not necessarily involve lifetime interests, but may exist only for the moment.

For instance, a young man wants more than anything to become a medical doctor. This is his long-range goal. But suppose you have a story in which he is accused of cheating on an exam. His goal within the story then could be to prove he didn't cheat. The antagonist may have the same long-term goal of becoming a physician. But he has framed the protagonist because they are in contest for a scholarship they both desperately need. The antagonist's goal within the story is to frame the other man.

It also helps to figure out motives if they are important. A motive sometimes is the same as a goal, sometimes different. In the example of the two men in medical school, the antagonist's goal was to frame the other man. His motive was to win the scholarship.

It is important to figure out the relationships among the characters. Taking the story of the two men in medical school, perhaps the protagonist looks upon the other person as a friend and feels close to him. This complicates things further because he may not then suspect him of being devious.

In "Whose Woods These Are," Roy has been close to his father, thinking him invincible. When he learns in a harsh way that the father indeed is far from invincible, it affects his relationships with everyone except his wife. He views everyone as an opponent.

Even if a story does not follow a plot, you need to figure out the important lines and actions that the audience needs to know to follow what you're saying overall.

Determining the Mood

Another aspect of your analysis is to determine both the predominate and the subordinate moods. What feeling is most important for the listener to experience once you finish telling your story? This is the predominant mood.

In a story in which you are pointing out a social problem, such as racial prejudice, the feeling you want the audience to experience may be determination (to eliminate this sort of prejudice). During the story itself, you may have other subordinate moods: sympathy with those discriminated against, outrage at the idea of prejudice, anger at the perpetrators of the discriminatory action, and so on.

Although the following is a poem instead of a story, I'm including it as a brief illustration of determining mood.

SONNET 30

by William Shakespeare

When to the Sessions of sweet silent thought
I summon up remembrance of things past,
I sigh the lack of many a thing I sought,
And with old woes new wail my dear time's waste.
Then can I drown an eye (unus'd to flow),
For precious friends hid in death's dateless night,
And weep afresh love's long since cancelled woe,
And moan the expense of many a vanished sight.
Then can I grieve at grievances foregone,
And heavily from woe to woe tell o'er
The sad account of fore-bemoaned moan,
Which I new pay, as if not paid before.
  But if the while I think on thee (dear friend),
  All losses are restored, and sorrows end.

At first glance it might seem that the predominate mood is nostalgia or sorrow. But on closer examination, you can determine that it's one of happiness because the narrator, though sorrowful throughout the first twelve lines, has only to think of the person to whom the poem was written, and the mood changes.

Universality

A story should posses universality. It should include truths or ideas to which the audience can relate and which should elicit a common response. In the broadest sense this means the story should appeal to all people, in all places, at all times. Of course, this is ridiculous. Cultures and time periods and values differ too much.

Rather, universality, as I'll use it, means that a story needs to relate to your listeners, or at least to the majority of them.

Most often, any story you develop or any you consider using would possess universality. This often goes without saying. Even science fiction stories about alien races in the far future need to have meaning for us here and now, or they will not be successful.

You have to be able to identify with likable or admirable characters who are experiencing the same kinds of emotions you and your listeners feel. If a story is too far outside your realm of experience, it will mean very little to you, and you will know this immediately.

It can be helpful to figure out exactly what truths the story contains. How is it universal? Is it because it portrays feelings of hate or wonder or disgust? If so, determine where this is most apparent and point it up by vocal change and so on.

Remember that no matter how cleverly written, if the story you choose to tell is lacking in universality, it's a pretty good bet it will be a flop.

Let's look again at "The Pleiades," by Jerine Watson-Miner.

There were five, gathered together. And they waited. Soft, muted sobs escaped from them now and again, and they occasionally dabbed at their moist redness with small, white cottony balls.

Stutter couldn't sit still. She kept lifting her feet, one after the other, and wringing two of her hands. Her nervous agitation irritated her sisters and her constant movement made the floor tremble.

"For God's sake, Stutter! Be still! We've got enough trouble as it is without being bounced up and down like a bunch of common Long-Legs!"

"I'm sorry, Scythe. It's just that I can't believe she's dead. She was so young! With so much to live for! Why doesn't Silo get here? She's never on time for anything!"

"She's too damned fat, that's why. She can't move fast enough. She never should've wound up near all that grain."

Quick to criticize, Sugar Cane was sleek and vain. She was the only sister living in the remote wilderness, and the rugged environment had honed her body into a lean hardness. She had also grown callous and intolerant.

"Shut up, Sugar. All I've heard since I got here was how YOU lived the farthest away, how YOU arrived first, and how YOU can't stay long because it's harvest time. You, you, you! Our baby sister has been killed and you sit there thinking only of your selfish self!"

"I'm not selfish, Stutter. I'm smart. And careful. If September had been half as careful, she wouldn't be dead. And we wouldn't have had to stop everything for this stupid meeting, and I could be getting my food while it's fresh."

"All right. Hush. That's enough. I won't stand for any more bickering. Besides, I think I feel Silo coming."

Shingle's voice carried a note of quiet authority. She was the oldest of the sisters and in command.

It's easy to see almost from the beginning that the sisters are nonhuman, yet we can identify with them. We've all felt the emotions they feel. We've been nervous, apprehensive, impatient, and so on. We've all bickered and witnessed others bickering. The situation, a death, is certainly universal.

Reading only that far into the story, and without other clues, you might be able to guess that the sisters are spiders, black widows, and they are sitting on a web, hence the reference to jumping up and down. Yet the author has given them traits and a situation with which we can identify.

Suggestion

Stories often leave many things unsaid but strongly implied. You need to determine what these things are and how you can be sure an audience infers them as well. This connotative meaning may be much stronger than the literal one. In "Balloons! Candy! Toys!" what the story implies about discipleship is much more important than the tale of a boy who follows a balloon man and then becomes a balloon man. In this particular story, the characters deliberately are not developed, nor do we know a great deal about the setting and the circumstances of the characters.

The author wrote the story this way because it suited his purpose more than would a story with completely three-dimensional characters and flushed out incidents.

Symbolism

In "Balloons! Candy! Toys!" the characters and their actions not only suggest something else, but actually are symbols for a leader, Jesus, and a disciple, whoever it might be. Were we to read this story in a secular magazine, we might not realize this. Yet most certainly we would know that the story is a parable, that is it contains an entire other meaning, and that the various aspects are symbols for that meaning.

A symbol is a device a writer uses to condense and to compare. It uses one thing to represent another.

Symbolism can be used in many ways, such as having the entire story mean something else, or it can be used by having things inside a story be representative of something else. In "Whose Woods These Are" Donald's throwing the father in the mud becomes a symbol of failure to the central character. In "Going Steady" the watch is a symbol both of the boy's heritage and of his grandmother's love for him, and it becomes a symbol, though untruthfully, that shows Karen and Martin now are a team.

Two common types of symbolism are metaphors and similes, each a means of comparison. Going back once again to "Whose Woods These Are," you can see various uses of metaphor (saying something actually is something else) and simile (saying something is like something else). One of the metaphors is: "A jetliner grazed the tops of buildings..." Actually, it didn't, or there would certainly have been bad if not disastrous results. This is simply a condensed way of saying that the plane appeared to Roy to graze the building, though he knew it didn't. It only came close.

Another example: "I had the world by its throat, threatening it into submission." This also anthropomorphizes the world, giving it human characteristics, and second it means that Roy was in control; he had become highly successful.

The foregoing are metaphors. A simile from the same story would be: "Kids who puff out their chests like banty roosters." The image this calls to mind is exact and more powerful than it would be simply to try to explain how they appeared and acted.

All of these things are important for a listener to grasp because they help to define and describe. Since they generally are short, there's a risk they may be missed. You need to decide how you can make sure the audience will follow them.

Imagery

Similes and metaphors are forms of imagery. But imagery is more than that. It is a word or group of words that relates to any of our senses, not just taste, smell, touch, hearing and sight, but to such things as our sense of movement, temperature, balance, thirst, hunger, and pain.

Perhaps more than any other factor in writing or storytelling, imagery stimulates the imagination. It brings about a blending of our experiences with the material in the story. It is a direct collaboration between the storyteller and the listener. Everyone's experiences differ from everyone else's. So when a writer or storyteller talks about a maple tree, each person can call up a mental image of that tree. But none of these images will be the same. Yet when you relate this image to your own experience, it makes the experience described in the story more interesting and more meaningful.

"Whose Woods These Are" is filled with imagery. For instance:

"...the outer walls great sheets of glass"—sight, perhaps temperature if you visualize sunlight on the glass.

"Sun sparkled on the rippling waves"—sight, temperature, movement.

"...the Coronado Bridge curved gracefully into the distance"—sight, perhaps even movement.

"...the stream, icy cold, that meandered behind the barn; the sun-drenched fields of wheat and corn, and, past the fields, the coolness of the sugar woods with its soft carpet of leaves. I remembered the sun casting dappled shadows through the maple trees; the grey squirrels, and the large-eyed does and spotted fawns"—sight, temperature, hearing the stream, movement of the stream and the wheat and corn, maybe even smell, and hearing in the leaves underfoot.

Imagery is one of the major factors in bringing a story to life.

Paraphrasing

Particularly if you are telling a story written by someone else, it's a good idea to try to paraphrase it to be certain that you do follow and understand it the whole way through.

If you follow all these steps in your analysis, you certainly have an edge in communicating well with your listener.

Eleven

Using Your Voice

Since your voice is so important to what you'll be doing, you'll want it to be as flexible as possible to use it to the fullest potential.

Certainly, some voices are more resonant and melodious than others. But it's what you do with the voice you have that's important.

There are four overall areas of voice usage. They are time, pitch, volume, and quality.

Time

Time can be broken into four subcategories, one of which is **rate.** This means the delivery speed of the presentation, or to put it differently, the number of words you utter per minute.

Some people naturally talk faster than others. This is to be expected. But often when people give a public presentation, they tend to go much too fast, usually because of nervousness or a feeling that they're dragging things out. Just as irritating is the person who speaks too slowly, with lots of vocal hesitations.

In storytelling there are times when you will want to vary your rate of speaking, and often this is instinctive. You know for instance that when people are excited they speak faster. In a somber frame of mind, their speech is slower.

The emotional content of your story has a bearing on the rate at which you tell it. You may even vary your rate to portray differences in the personalities of the characters. One may be very deliberate in thought and speech, while another forges ahead without stopping to consider exact words and phrases.

In the character analysis and in determining the subordinate moods, you can figure out the feelings of the piece and how to portray them.

The thought content of the story also should affect the rate of delivery. You would present a nostalgic or reflective scene more slowly than one that is intended to be funny. If the ideas require concentration, you also would deliver them more slowly than you would simple ideas.

Another aspect of timing is **duration,** which refers to the length of each individual sound, and, like rate, depends on the emotions you present. It also depends on the importance of individual words and phrases. This then is one way you can point up or emphasize important words or ideas.

When you are analyzing your story, you should try to determine not only the important words but the thought centers as well. This means analyzing exactly what the character is saying so you know the important words and word groups. A thought center is a complete image or concept, though not usually a complete sentence.

In the following selection, the excerpt from "The Cup" that appeared earlier, I've alternated italicizing with boldfacing to show word groups. Words that are not of particular importance appear in regular type. Once you have figured out the word groups, if you are presenting a written story word for word, this is simply another means of helping you decide which parts are most important. In choosing the word groups, skip over unimportant words so they are not emphasized when you tell the story.

> It was a *winter day* sewn with the *thread of pain,* sewn to a **tattered autumn** at *one end* and to an as yet **unshrunk spring** *on the other*—a **winter** which **lingered** too long, so that the *gray* of the *clouds* cast **musty shadows** on *everyone's spirit.*

You can emphasize a word or phrase with still another device, **pausing.** Any time you use a deliberate pause, you are telling the audience that they should listen closely to what is to follow.

The next time you see a comedian on television, pay attention to when the person uses pauses. Most often, there will be one before a punchline. You often hear it said that a comedian has a good sense of timing. Generally, this means the person has a good sense of pausing.

Briefer pauses also provide a kind of oral punctuation. If you were to tell your story at an even rate, the audience simply wouldn't be able to follow. After a sentence or so, your story would begin to sound like gibberish. Yet you certainly should not pause every time there is written punctuation. If you do, the speech will be choppy and uneven.

A third purpose for using pauses is to determine phrasing. In a certain degree, this is an individual matter, and there is no "correct" style to use. Phrasing depends on the style of the story, your own personal style, and the emotional and logical content of the story. The following sentence would be delivered quickly, pausing only briefly when at all. This is to create verbally a sense of rushing and maybe panic:

> John was frantic. He rushed from room to room, giving everything only a cursory glance, before running into the garage and jumping into the car.

You might say this sentence with a very brief pause after the word "room," and one after "glance," although you wouldn't even need the second pause. On the other hand, the following sentence would require longer and more frequent pauses:

> "Dear God," he prayed, "please, please let her be all right. I can't live without her. I simply can't live without her. So...so if you spare her life, I promise..." His voice broke. "Oh, God, I won't ever, ever hurt her again."

To convey the character's emotional state, you probably would want a kind of choppiness, as if it's very difficult for him to get out the words, to admit to whatever he's done. You have to convey the idea that although the man apparently hurt the other person, he realizes how important she is. As I said, the phrasing is an individual thing. So the following is only one way of presenting the material. A single slash mark indicates a relatively short pause, a double slash mark a longer pause, and the triple slash a long pause.

> "Dear God," // he prayed, / "please, // please / let her be / all right. /// I can't live without her. I / simply / can't // live without her. /// So... // so if you // spare her life, I // promise..." /// His voice broke. /

"Oh, God, // I won't / ever, // ever / hurt her //
again."

Were you to present the material as indicated, along
with using other devices, it would indicate a person
near the point of a mental breakdown. But you might
want to present it from a more objective point of view,
as the storyteller standing back from the characters.
Then you might do it something like this.

"Dear God," he prayed, / "please, // please let her
be all right. I can't live without her. // I simply can't
/ live without her. So... // so if you spare her life, I //
promise..." // His voice broke. / "Oh, God, / I won't
ever, ever / hurt her again."

The last aspect of timing is **rhythm**. A humorous
piece or pithy story might have a staccato rhythm,
whereas a more somber story would have a more flow-
ing language. The rhythm has to match the style and
content. Rhythm also involves the recurrence of a
word, an idea, a sound, or a pattern of sounds. Examine how each of the following flows and then compare how the pieces differ from each other.

More swiftly than light they journeyed through
the corridors of space until at last they reached the
light force Olanthros-Tau.
This star, like nearly all others they passed, held a
score of whirling captives under its influence. One
of them, Behazi as it was called, was considerably
larger than the others, holding under its own
power eleven moons. The cloud-wrapped seventh,
their destination, appeared from afar like a soft ball
of whitest cotton (David Edman, *Once Upon an
Eternity*, chapter 7).

"You poor darlings," Ramey-Do was telling them.
"Treated so! Driven from your home! Frightened
half out of your wits by these vagabonds! Sent
packing God-knows where! And if that weren't
enough, they've gone and taken your *food* away!
Not even a tiny morsel to sustain you! Why, it's
hardly fair, if you ask me!"

"Karam-Bor, they're *listening* to him!" Trazel
whispered urgently. "They're taking it all *in*!"

"It's starting already, I regret to say," Karam-Bor
replied.

"What is starting?"

"A rebellion. A stupid, petty little rebellion"
(Edman, *Eternity*, chapter 9).

As summer grows heavy with life and warm
afternoons begin to smell of autumn, children grow
bored as they splash in shallow puddles of stagnant
time (Joseph J. Juknialis, "Carved Out of Love and
Shaped into Seasons," *When God Began in the
Middle*).

The first excerpt has an even narrative rhythm. The
second is less even because it is a scene of conflict. The
third has a poetic rhythm.

Volume

Similar to rate of speaking, volume is determined in
part by the mood of your story. You probably would
convey frustration or anger at a higher decibel level
than you would serenity. Volume is also determined
by the size of your audience and by the physical surroundings. You'd speak more loudly to a large group
than to a small one and more softly in an enclosed
space than in a park.

Increased volume can point up or emphasize. In the
following I've boldfaced the words that you would

speak more loudly. And remember that when you emphasize anything, you use a combination of verbal devices. You might pause ahead of time and then speak the word slowly.

> "What **then?** What **happened** to her?" Silo's voice **choked** with new **tears** as she looked to Shingle for an answer.
> "That's why I **Wire-Throbbed** everyone to come here. **All** of us are needed." Shingle drew herself up tall, stiffening her cephalothorax for emphasis. "It was an **unprovoked, unwarranted attack** from an enemy heretofore unsuspected. The **Farm Woman** killed her, Silo!!"
> "The **Farm Woman?** You must be **mistaken!**"

Here I boldfaced the most important words in the story for emphasis, much like picking out the thought centers. But more than that, such words as "Farm Woman" and "unwarranted attack" show, partially through increased volume, the shock and outrage of the sisters. The excerpt, of course, is from Jerine Watson-Miner's "The Pleiades."

Pitch

Pitch, changes in the frequency of sound, is another effective way of communicating meaning. When a sound is spoken at a higher pitch level than other words in a phrase, it has attention called to it. Generally, changes in pitch are accompanied by one or more of the other devices used to point things up. Go back to the example from "The Pleiades." Try to say the words in a monotone, that is at the same pitch level, using only an increase in volume for emphasis. Now try to say the same excerpt increasing the volume *and* raising the pitch level at the same time.

Changes in pitch not only occur from word to word, but within individual words. The latter, of course, is called inflection. There are no hard and fast rules that work in every situation, but a rising inflection often conveys a question, a sense of doubt, or a sense of disbelief or shock. A falling inflection can signal determination or certainty. Abrupt changes from falling to rising or vice versa can show confusion or bewilderment.

Vocal Quality

Quality refers to the changes in the overtones in one's voice when speaking. Changes in quality can be used to indicate changes in meaning, to portray certain emotions, or to indicate that a different character is speaking. Most often it is associated with mood and feeling. For example, let's once again look at Jerine Watson-Miner's "The Pleiades" to see how both the personality of the sisters and the emotions they are feeling can be communicated through the use of different vocal qualities.

> They were five, gathered together. And they waited. Soft, muted sobs escaped from them now and again, and they occasionally dabbed at their moist redness with small, white cottony balls.
> Shutter couldn't sit still. She kept lifting her feet, one after the other, and wringing two of her hands. Her nervous agitation irritated her sisters and her constant movement made the floor tremble.
> "For God's sake, Shutter! Be still! We've got enough trouble as it is without being bounced up and down like a bunch of common Long-Legs!" [The quality here could show sternness; there would be a lack of overtones.]

> "I'm sorry, Scythe. It's just that I can't believe
> she's dead. She was so young! With so much to live
> for! Why doesn't Silo get here? She's never on time
> for anything!" [Probably a whining quality, and
> maybe a hint of a breathy quality to indicate that
> she is emotionally a little girl.]
>   "She's too damned fat, that's why. She can't move
> fast enough. She never should've wound up near
> all that grain. [Harsh quality.]

A gruff or husky quality may indicate an intense depth of feeling, such as sorrow, whereas a whining quality is often associated with pleading. The use of various vocal qualities depends a great deal on how you want to tell the story, that is, whether to use the objective or performance approach or a combination.

There is a great deal to remember so far as voice usage is concerned. Much of it comes naturally or without a lot of thought.

Vocal Production[1]

Not everyone can have deep, mellow voices, but unless there is some physiological cause, you should be able to develop an effective voice for storytelling.

The first prerequisite of good vocal production is proper breathing. Even though we have been breathing all our lives, we do not necessarily do it correctly.

Many of us have a tendency to breathe largely with the chest. This shallow type of breathing usually is more than adequate to sustain us through our daily ac-

---

1. The material on voice production articulation is in large part
    excerpted from: Marsh Cassady, *Acting Step-by-Step*,
    (Resource Publications: San Jose, 1988). See Chapter 7, "The
    Voice," for a more complete discussion of the subject.

tivities. And it is closest to the "proper" type of breathing for running or jogging when we need a quick supply of fresh oxygen, which shallow breathing fulfills.

For any activity in which you have to project your voice, you need to breathe in a different way, to have better control of the air passing in and out of your lungs. Many people have a tendency to speak or sing "from the throat" rather than from the lungs, when they are running out of air.

To produce sound, the vocal folds vibrate when a column of air passes through them. It's a fairly automatic process; the vocal folds adjust as you want them to. Yet if you attempt to project your voice without breathing properly, you tense your throat, trying to "squeeze" out the sound. This can result in a husky quality or even laryngitis.

To relax the tension in the throat, let your jaw drop open. Produce an "ahhh" without trying to focus or project, and don't worry about how you sound. Pay attention to how you feel, and then try to carry the relaxed feeling over to other voiced sounds. Relaxed humming also is good.

What is proper breathing for speech? Generally, it is the way we breathe when we are lying down. We take in larger quantities of air, filling the abdomen and the chest, inhaling and exhaling an unobstructed flow of air.

To learn to breathe in this way, try lying on your back. Push as hard as you can against your abdomen with the palms of your hands. Suddenly release the abdomen, and the air should flow in. Now try the same thing standing up. Keep trying till it becomes second nature to breathe deeply when you are telling a story.

One of the best aids to good voice production and projection is good posture, which supports your vocal mechanism and gives it room to operate in an effective manner. You need to use your resonators to their best advantage. Resonators are those parts of the body that provide amplification for the voice, like the tubing of a brass instrument or the sounding board of a piano. They include the throat, nose, and mouth, as well as the bones in the head and the chest. Their purpose is to enrich and reinforce the original tone.

The more relaxed the throat, the more pleasant and full the resonation. Tension may cause undesirable voice qualities, such as whininess or breathiness. Speaking at improper pitch also affects resonation and can tire or damage the voice.

To determine if you are speaking at the proper pitch level, use a piano to assist in seeing how high and how low you can sing comfortably without strain. Some people, of course, will have much broader ranges than others. This doesn't really matter as far as speaking is concerned.

Count how many notes in your range and divide by four. A fourth of the way from the bottom should be your "habitual pitch," the note you hit most often in speaking. To see if that is the case, simply start to talk and sustain one of the notes rather than cutting it off. You won't always hit the same note, nor should you try. You should be speaking within the range of this particular note, higher or lower depending on such factors as emotional content or situation.

Just as the body needs to be relaxed and warmed up, so does the voice. If you've taken singing lessons, you probably are acquainted with warmup exercises that can help your speaking voice as well. The following can help:

1. Stretch the jaw as much as you can, pulling it from side to side.

2. Yawn two or three times to open up the throat.

3. Exhale as sharply as you can and then let the air rush back in.

Articulation

Another aspect of voice usage is articulation, the forming of consonants using the lips, teeth, tongue, alveolar ridge, hard and soft palates, and glottis. The way these are positioned, as far as contact or near contact with one another, determines the particular sound. Slight differences account for regional dialects or accents. Vast differences, whether physiological or out of habit, result in unintelligible speech.

You should learn to speak clearly without emphasizing the sound so much that it calls attention to itself. The generally accepted dialect in the United States is called Mid-American Standard, and is pretty typical of the Midwest, without the twang. Nearly all newscasters speak in the generally accepted way. If you are not sure of your own speech, try tuning into the evening news and matching the speech patterns used there to your own.

It has often been said that Americans have sloppy speech habits. This means they are lazy about proper articulation. It's easier to pronounce a "d" rather than a "t" in words such as "better," or to say "probly" instead of "probably." It's easier to say "tick" for "thick" or "dis" for "this." When you are practicing the telling of your story, devote one of the "tellings" to paying attention to your articulation. Unless you have a speech handicap, you should with more practice be able to correct yourself.

Twelve

Using Your Body

Your body constantly communicates thoughts and feelings. You communicate much more nonverbally than with the use of words. This nonverbal communication should complement or add to the overall effect of your storytelling. There are five important ways in which you use your body to communicate: eye contact, gestures, facial expression, stance, and movement from place to place. Depending on the situation in which you are telling a story, there may be two more: physical contact and spatial distances.

With your body you reveal your personality, show how you are feeling and even give clues as to whether or not you are telling the truth. This is called body language, generally a neglected area until the past few years.

Overall, we have been taught what certain body language means, such as nodding and shrugging. But many signs are much more subtle.

When you are telling a story to an audience, you need to communicate what goes along with the story

133

rather than give contradictory signs that indicate nervousness. You know these signs as well as anyone—playing with a button, twisting your hair, looking down at the floor. You need to train yourself to be aware of this sort of thing. Often, simply by being aware of behavior like this, you can eliminate it.

Of course, we are all individuals, and we project our individuality. A storyteller cannot divorce personality completely from the presentation. Yet, he or she can work to see that these individual idiosyncrasies do not distract from the storytelling.

Eye Contact

A person who has eye contact with his or her listeners comes across as forthright and honest.

It is important to look at your listeners so they know you really are interested in them and in telling your story for them to hear.

By looking at the audience, you will remain aware of the communication process. Even though you are the only one speaking, communication with an audience is not a one-way street. An audience responds, maybe not with words but nonverbally.

Simply by glancing at them, you can tell if they're bored or interested. If they're bored, it's a good bet that you're doing something to obstruct your purpose. When you are in direct contact, you will know this and can try to analyze what you are doing wrong and then change it.

However, there are times during the story when you may not want to look at the listeners, particularly when you are using a performance approach and actually portraying rather than indicating the characters. Yet in the narrative parts, this can change, so you again look at the listeners.

Gestures

There are four types of gestures: 1) directive or indicative; 2) descriptive; 3) expressive or emphatic; and 4) private or self-communicative.

The first includes such things as pointing, shrugging, or shaking the head. This type is generally accepted and unvarying within a particular culture. Everyone knows what these gestures mean.

The second type is less exact, though when accompanied with words, is usually self-apparent. We raise an arm and say, "He's about this tall." We spread our index finger and thumb and say, "I came this close to running right into her."

The third type gesture is used for emphasis. We pound a fist into our palm to show anger. We shrug. These are fairly accurate indications of how we feel. But without words, it is difficult to tell what they relate to.

The last type is meant only for self, although the gesture may be the same one we use to communicate to someone else. We drum our fingers on a table top. We slump and sigh. Gestures like this show reactions to our environment, but they are nonspecific. Drumming the fingers, for instance, can show impatience or nervousness. Without words people observing you could see you were reacting, but out of context, they wouldn't be able to tell what you were reacting against. You have to be the most careful about this kind of gesture when you tell an audience stories because this type can take you unaware and communicate things not connected with the story.

The gestures need to fit the emotional content, the characters, and the circumstances of the story.

There are a few other things to consider about gestures. First, are they natural to you? Do you feel comfortable with them? If not, don't use them. Some people just naturally use a lot of gestures; other's don't. It's better not to use gestures than to try to force them.

Along the same lines, you need to use your whole body for a gesture. Nothing looks phonier than to see someone point only with the arm, without "stepping into" the gesture. The more comfortable you feel with gestures, the more natural they will appear. The more experience you have telling stories to groups, the more comfortable you will become. Consequently, gestures may then begin to be easier for you.

Another thing to remember is that the size of the gesture increases with the size of the audience.

Facial Expressions

The more exaggerated the story and your presentation, the more exaggerated the facial expressions should be. If you are telling a story just for fun, the facial expressions can be broad.

Overall, facial expressions are more subtle than other types of body language used in storytelling. This is because from several rows back they are hard to discern. Of course, if you can be seen clearly by every one of your listeners, your facial expressions can be an effective complement to your storytelling. Your face can reflect a wide range of emotions from joy to anger. If you smile, the audience can determine, for instance, that what you are saying should not be taken seriously, or that you are portraying a kindly mood. In other words, facial expressions can give the audience clues as to how the story is intended. Through a combination of facial expression and other body language, listeners can easily discern emotions and states of being, such as tiredness, depression, happiness and so on.

Stance

It's easy to tell that a person who slumps and hangs his or her head is in a negative mood, and that someone who stands with crossed arms probably isn't pleased and doesn't want to carry on a friendly conversation. On the other hand, if someone is sitting on the edge of a stage, leaning back slightly, using his or her arms as props, you'd probably infer openness and expansiveness.

The same is true when you tell a story in front of a group. As is the case with other types of body language, you need to be aware of what you are conveying and what you want to convey through the way you stand and carry yourself.

Movement from Place to Place

You can communicate happiness by a springy step, sadness by walking slowly, nervousness by taking fast, jerky steps. If you are using a performance approach, you not only can move in a characteristic way for each person in the story, but you can shift slightly from one location to another so your listener knows you are switching characters. For instance, if you face slightly to the left and then shift to face to the right, the audience will understand that now a new character is speaking.

If you step from one place to another, it also can show that you are beginning a new section of the story. It tells the audience that now you've finished that part and are ready to go on to something else.

The more distance between you and your audience, the more emotionally remote you seem. Far away, you seem to set up a barrier. The closer you are, the more intimate or the more it indicates a willingness to share yourself and your story. Touching, of course, is the most intimate of all. These things depend on the situation, the place you're telling the story, its purpose, and your listeners.

Thirteen

An Analysis of a Story: "The Gift"

I wrote the following story in 1963. I'll try to go through all the steps of analyzing it, just as if I were going to tell it before an audience.

THE GIFT

by Marsh Cassady

It was cold that night in the hills above Bethlehem. Biting wind whipped through the folds of my woolen robe. My teeth chattered as I tried to hug the warmth of the smoldering fire. Wood was scarce, and I didn't dare leave the sheep.

It was my first season as a shepherd. I'd been there at various times before but always with Father. Now he was getting too old to spend his days following the sheep.

I didn't really mind too much. I felt a sense of pride in being entrusted with the responsibility of keeping the flock. Now I knew Father no longer looked upon me as a child. I was growing up, becoming a man.

I wanted to be a good shepherd as my Father had been. But sometimes I became discouraged. It was very lonesome there with only Joab and Zach to keep me company. They were both much younger than my seventeen years, and I always let them sleep while I took the night watch.

At times like that—late at night when the earth was still and the dark sky pierced by tiny lights—I'd climb to the highest peak above Bethlehem. There I had a special rock where I'd sit, my arms wrapped around my knees, gazing at the village below. I'd think of my friends who lived there—Jacob, son of the tentmaker, and Samuel, the fisherman's son. I envied the boys their sports and games, their idle hours of listening to old Saul playing the pipes.

Not that I didn't have idle hours. But what could I do with them? Picture the time when I'd have a flock of sheep of my own—not a small one like Father's, but a large one that would take twenty shepherds to watch. Then I'd spend my nights at the inn in the village, or I'd travel. I'd always wanted to visit the exotic places described by the occasional sojourner who stopped for lodging in the village.

My dreams were a way of passing the time, but it wasn't very likely they'd come to pass. Times were hard, and Jews, like myself, weren't allowed to advance very far. Also Caesar Augustus had just sent out a new tax decree—much worse than the last.

Actually, mine wasn't such a bad lot. My family was better off than many. Poor Joab and Zach had nothing. Their father was a helpless invalid, whom their mother had to wait on constantly. The meager pay Father could give the boys was all the money the family had.

But these thoughts still didn't make it less cold or remedy my need for company. Maybe, just maybe, it wouldn't hurt anything if I walked over to the next hill to talk with old John, the ancient shepherd who watched the flocks of Azor.

I always enjoyed listening to the stories he told—of the time a band of robbers tried to steal his sheep and how he fought them off with nothing but his staff; of the time the entire flock was afflicted by a strange pestilence which threatened to kill them all; or of the time he rescued the young shepherd who'd been attacked by a pack of savage beasts.

As I started walking, a light suddenly appeared, making the night as bright as mid-day. I clapped my hands to my eyes and fell to the ground. Was God venting his punishment against me for thinking frivolous thoughts, for neglecting my duties?

No, it couldn't be. I was only an unimportant shepherd boy, doubtless thinking the same thoughts as many before me.

A warm breeze brushed my face. I felt a gentle touch on my forehead. Daring to look up, I saw the most beautiful creature ever beheld by Man. He was an angel with wings as white as the fleece of a newborn lamb. His face held a look of purest love.

He said to me: "Fear not: for behold I bring you good tidings of great joy; which shall be to all people. For unto you is born this day in the city of David a Savior, which is Christ the Lord.

"And this shall be a sign unto you. Ye shall find the babe wrapped in swaddling clothes, lying in a manger."

And then with the angel there was a great multitude of others, singing and praising God.

As suddenly as they appeared, they were gone. I began to doubt they were ever there. Maybe I was alone too much. But what about the newborn Babe? If He was real, then I'd know. I looked about me. Shepherds on nearby knolls appeared bewildered too. Then they'd also witnessed the strange spectacle.

Quickly, I ran to Joab and Zach and shook their shoulders. "Did you hear? Did you see?" I asked.

"Leave me alone," Zach complained.

Joab opened an eye and squinted at my face. "What do you want? Is it time to get up?"

"Then you didn't hear. You didn't see. Oh, it was beautiful. An angel of God appeared to me and told me about a Savior—a Savior born tonight in a stable in Bethlehem."

Zach nudged Joab and winked. "Go back to sleep, Jeremiah. I'll take over if you can't stay awake."

"But it's true, I tell you. It is!"

"Sure," said Zach.

"All right. If you don't believe me, go see for yourselves. Go into Bethlehem and seek out the stable."

"He won't give up, will he, Zach?" Joab said. "I'll tell you what, Jeremiah. You go. Now that we're awake, we'll watch the sheep. Won't we, Zach?"

"No! That wouldn't be fair."

"Go. Find out for yourself it was only a dream."

"Well...all right."

I couldn't believe my good fortune. I would be one of the first to see the Savior. Me, Jeremiah! The shepherd boy.

Before they could change their minds I raced down the hill. It was a long way. By the time I reached the bottom I was gasping for breath.

Maybe I was being silly. Why would the Savior be born in a stable? I must be losing my mind. Where would I go anyway? What stable would hold a Holy Child?

I saw a group of shepherds a short distance ahead. Perhaps they knew where the stable was. I hurried to join them as they turned a corner onto one of the narrow streets of Bethlehem.

"Wait," I yelled. The men stopped and turned. When I reached them, I wanted to ask about the Baby. But I was afraid of what they might think. Finally, I blurted, "Are you...I mean, did you see..."

One of the older men laughed and placed a hand on my shoulder. "Yes, boy, we saw what you did. We're on our way now to observe this miracle." Gently, he pushed me in front of him. "Let us not delay."

The shepherds seemed to know where they were going. They continued down the street toward the stable behind the only inn in Bethlehem. Already a group of men were gathering near the door. As we approached, they began to go inside.

I don't know what I expected but certainly not what I saw. The rough wooden floor was covered with bits of hay. An overpowering odor of animal dung filled the air. To the left were a dozen or more stalls where donkeys pawed the ground and snorted puffs of white air. It was even colder here than outside.

I crept closer to the front. The Baby lay on a bed of straw in one of the stalls. His mother lay beside Him, cuddling Him, as the father, a tall, bearded man, stood nearby, breathing on his knobby hands to make them warm.

There was nothing unusual about the Baby. He was just a little boy, born into a world of cold and hunger. His fine, brown hair was still damp from the birth. There was no halo around His head as some of the shepherds were heard to say later. His tiny hands looked blue, and His face was puckered up as if He were about to cry.

I don't know what possessed me, but suddenly I shrugged out of my robe. Creeping forward with outstretched hand, I thrust it at the woman, whom the man addressed as Mary. Her eyes filled with tears as she laid it gently over the Baby. I stood there a second more, then turned and raced outside.

What had I done? What would Mother say when she discovered my robe was gone? She'd spent hours making it. She said she wanted me to have something special to take with me to the hills. It was a beautiful, dark blue robe, woven so there were no seams. It was the warmest—and the nicest—I'd ever seen.

Now I had nothing. Nothing to keep me warm. I'd freeze up there one of these cold nights. Suddenly, I realized something. Though others around me huddled together and beat their arms against their sides, I wasn't cold at all. The warmth I was experiencing seemed to start deep inside me and spread outward until it encompassed my entire body.

I had to get back to the sheep. It wasn't right to leave Zach and Joab by themselves. Besides I was eager to tell someone what I'd witnessed.

By the time I got back I was so cold I couldn't control my shaking. It must have been the excitement that had made me feel warm. I borrowed a ragged, burlap robe from old John, who said he kept it around just in case someone needed it.

That night was the last time I ever saw my robe. Neither was I fortunate enough ever again to see the Christ, though I heard many stories of His preaching and teaching. I didn't get my large flock of sheep either, but I'm comfortable enough. Right now I'm teaching my own son to take over my duties.

A short while back I was very saddened to hear of our Savior's crucifixion—for I did come to believe He is the true Savior.

I heard another story too. About a robe. It is said the Christ wore a robe to Calvary, and the soldiers cast lots for it. It was a magnificent garment, woven so well there were no seams.

I like to believe it was the robe I... But no, it couldn't be. No garment would last that long. I'm getting to be an old man now, entitled to dream a bit—just as that seventeen-year-old boy did thirty-three years ago on the hills above the City of David.

THE END

First, I choose the people who will hear it: a group of friends gathered for the Christmas holidays. What do I know about these people? Why do I want to tell them a story? Part of the reason is that I want to recapture, both for myself and for others, the innocence of the time when it was written. I was twenty-seven years old. My wife, Pat, and I had two little girls, ages three and two.

Times were rough. We had little money; we'd bought a house, beyond what we really could afford. I wanted to give Pat something special for Christmas. I decided to write a book just for her. I'd have to do it in secret because I wouldn't want her to suspect.

My book contained pages of poetry, a song I'd composed, and three stories, one of which is terribly outdated now. All the hours I spent were well worth it to see the look of surprise and love and happiness on the face of my wife when she opened the gift.

Now I'd like to give the same gift once more. Thomas Wolfe wrote that you can't go home again. And I know that to be true. My wife has been dead since 1978, so telling the story will be bittersweet. I can't go home, but I can remember.

Who are these friends? People with whom I'm comfortable. People, who like me, have probably become much too cynical. People who doubt too much. If that's the case then, won't I be taking a risk in reading this sort of story?

It's not the literal story so much I want them to hear, though that's important too, but the idea that we have to have faith in something. So okay, I'll go ahead and do it. And if I do, what sort of an introduction should I use?

How about some of the things I've been thinking? About doing this story so long ago, about missing my wife, missing my two oldest kids, one of whom I didn't even get to see for six years. The book was about them too. About taking them shopping, about their choosing their own presents for Mom. There was a purity then, that I miss. I'll take the risk and say this. If they're really my friends, and I know they are, they'll understand.

So okay. I'll make the introduction spontaneous. I'll point to the picture frame above the mantle. It contains a centerfold that is a Christmas photo and features one of the poems from the book, and maybe I'll make a joke about always being ahead of my time. Although I wrote the "book" all those years ago, that poem and two of the stories were published only within the last few years.

That will lead into the book, and why it means so much.

What will the setting be like? Is there anything I have to anticipate that will be out of the ordinary? Well, it will be my living room, so that's no problem. Except it will be different than standing in front of a group of people. We'll all be sitting around; the tree will be up. I'll sit on the low mantle by the fireplace. Very informal.

How will I tell the story? Actually, I think I'll read it, even though I know it pretty well. I can't just tell it as a third-person narrator because so much depends on its being told from the shepherd's point of view, his experience, intimate.

What about the story itself? The theme? Do I remember? Or all those years ago, did I just want to do a story and not think of what it meant?

Actually, I wanted it to deal with the *real* Christmas, the spirit of Christmas. I can't just dwell on the idea of "lost innocence." I didn't mean that then. Our whole lives were ahead of us.

What I meant, what the story says, is: things work out. No matter how bad they seem, they work out. You have to have faith in that. That's what the story says literally; the boy never became wealthy. But he did okay. Pat and I would do okay. But we didn't. There were all those debts when I went to graduate school...and then she got sick and died. But I can't think about that if I want to be true to the story. Still, it's bound to have an effect.

Does it have a plot? It doesn't seem to. The first part is description and setting, narration about the boy and his family and the other shepherds. It shows his dissatisfaction, and his guilt in realizing he's better off than many.

Then I had to get in some socioeconomic stuff and background about what things were like in general back at the time of Jesus' birth. The tax and so on.

Even a third of the way into the story, there's no real conflict. It's more a story of idea than of plot. There's some tension when Jeremiah sees the light and the angel speaks with him, but it really isn't an inciting incident.

There are some struggle and conflict later. Maybe an inciting incident of a sort is when Jeremiah decides that he has to go see if what the angel said is true. There's the complication then of knowing he should stand guard, but the other boys tell him it's okay to leave. Until then he was so certain of what he saw and heard, but now he isn't too sure. That complication is solved when he meets the shepherds at the bottom of the hill, and they verify what happened.

So there isn't a plot. There is a happening that creates a little bit of doubt and struggle, but it's easily solved. It's more an episode. "A day in the life of Jeremiah, the shepherd boy."

There's the harsh reality of the coldness of the stable, and the Baby, and Jeremiah's witnessing the scene. And by now we're more than two-thirds of the way through the story.

But then there's a definite complication when Jeremiah sees how cold the Baby is and gives him his robe. This is the high point of the story. Jeremiah's gift makes him feel good about himself, even though he worries about what his mother will think. Still, he knows he's done the right thing. He even begins to believe that the Savior performed a miracle in keeping him from feeling the cold.

In a little while, though, he knows it was the just the "heat" of the moment. The rest is falling action, a wrapping up of things, except for Jeremiah's wanting to believe Jesus kept the gift all His earthly life.

See, it is a story of faith and optimism. Jeremiah never advanced in status beyond what would have been normal, but he accepted that. Even more. He was content with it. And because of that one simple act, the giving of his gift, he could always feel good about himself.

It's one of those "pleasant" kinds of stories where not a great deal happens to cause a struggle, and where no one is really opposed, and where everything turns out right.

So how will I present it? I already decided I have to do it from Jeremiah's point of view, looking back. So I can't stand apart from it then. I have to become Jeremiah, as the older man. I have to be convincing. I have to analyze what he's like.

Well, he's a middle-aged man, fifty now, old for that historical period. He's probably a kindly person, understanding. He's proud of his own sons, glad he can teach them to follow in his footsteps. He knows it isn't the best of worlds. But it's far from the worst. In other words, he's a nice guy, a man who's made his peace with himself and his life.

How would he speak? Warmly, possibly a little hesitantly because he wouldn't be well-educated. When he told about the angel, his voice would have a sense of wonder. He'd show a little impatience with the two boys who won't believe him. Maybe, his voice would break when he talks about seeing the Baby Jesus. I don't want to overdo it.

Actually, he's a pretty easy character to analyze. A simple person, whose goal is to be a success. But he redefines what that means. At first, it means riches and being able to spend time at the inn, being able to travel. But as time goes on, he knows these things aren't so important. Success is really happiness.

What is the predominant mood? The feeling I'm left with? Gee, that's a hard one. There are so many feelings. Satisfaction, joy, a little sadness since Jeremiah is old now. You can't go home again, huh? Is that it? Yeah, but I think it's more a bittersweet feeling. I think the predominant mood is bittersweet.

And throughout the story, there are other feelings. Dissatisfaction, astonishment and wonder, excitement, doubt. I already figured all that out. But I have to keep it in mind as I practice.

I'll figure out the pausing, and the things to be emphasized. I've been doing this kind of thing for so many years I don't really write it out anymore. But I think it all through. And I go over and over the story, even though it's for a group of friends. Maybe that's more important to me personally than most audiences can be. I want to do it right. Let's see, I'll sit there and...

Oh, yeah, at the end, I'll ask if anyone wants to say anything. Ask me anything. I always do that. I try to do that. It's important. Well, it will be fun. I'll really enjoy it.

The foregoing is pretty much what I do when I tell a story, though, of course, the approach may be different. I don't really write all these things out anymore, but I do take the time to think them through. Actually, what I've shown you is my process, in a kind of stream-of-consciousness way.

I tried to be perfectly honest about the story, about my feelings for it and all that it means. It happens to be very personal. I usually tell or read my own stories, so to a degree they're all somewhat personal, though not so much as this one is.

When you tell a story, you probably will do better if you go through this process, even taking it further, marking the work for pauses and emphasis. In the margins of the manuscript, you can make notes to yourself on how you want to tell the story. Of course, you may not even use a manuscript when you actually go before an audience. But in the initial stages it will help you to be certain you've covered all the bases.

So, what are you waiting for? Go on and create some worlds.

Appendix

Whose Woods These Are

WHOSE WOODS THESE ARE

by Marsh Cassady

There comes a time in the lives of most men, I suppose, when they look back, assess where they've been, look to where they're going—and ask themselves: Is this all there is?

I was sitting in my office building—hell, one of my office buildings—the outer walls great sheets of glass, looking out over San Diego Bay. I'd just been going over figures, production costs, salaries, maintenance for an electronics plant I thought I might buy out.

Sun sparkled on the rippling waves; the Coronado Bridge curved gracefully into the distance. A jetliner grazed the tops of buildings to land at Lindberg Field. Thirty years ago I wanted to get as far away as I could, away from the hills of Western Pennsylvania, away from Grandpa's farm. I'd come to the furthest corner of California.

In less than ten years, I had the world by its throat, threatening it into submission. Now I'd begun to suspect that there was more to life than conquest.

I clasped my hands behind my head, leaned back in my chair. Living as I did, a person made few friends. Thank God I had Annabelle; she always stood by me.

I buzzed my secretary and told her to book a flight for Annabelle and me to Pennsylvania.

In Pittsburgh we rented a car and drove east on the Turnpike, my first time home in ages. There'd been no reason for returning. Dad had been dead a dozen years; Mom was in a nursing facility in Chula Vista.

Home? I asked myself. What did I mean by that? As a youngster, I felt that Grandpa's farm was more my home than the town where I was born and lived. I remembered the stream, icy cold, that meandered behind the barn; the sun-drenched fields of wheat and corn, and, past the fields, the coolness of the sugar woods with its soft carpet of fallen leaves. I remembered the sun casting dappled shadows through the maple trees; the grey squirrels, and the large-eyed does and spotted fawns.

These were the only memories that seemed "right." The others didn't fit. It was as if they belonged to someone else, to another person than the boy I used to be. I remembered the four-room house where the boy lived. I remembered his triumphs, his defeats. I remembered his father, his mother. But only the farm was completely mine.

That evening we found a motel, just off the Turnpike. Annabelle and I made love, delighting in each other's bodies as we hadn't in years.

We were in Somerset, nearly home. The next morning she would explore the town and do a little shopping. I'd go to Grandpa's farm alone.

"Are you sure you'll be okay?" I asked as I dropped her off.

"Of course," she said. "You do what you have to do." It was late September. She wore an amber-colored dress, shoes with straps that wound around her ankles, a silky scarf that made a pony tail of her raven hair. "I can't expect you to understand," I said. "I don't understand myself."

We'd arranged that I'd meet her at one up on the hill in front of the courthouse.

I headed north till I came to the old Lincoln Highway, Route 30. This was familiar territory. I'd learned to drive on these roads. I turned off at Kantner, followed the old dirt road.

I knew the farm had changed. The property was sold to a strip mining company that had gone broke before they could despoil the land. No one had lived there since Grandpa died while I was still in college.

The bridge over the stream—my stream—was new, but the house was a broken hull.
Weather-beaten grey, it sagged, the windows gone, a pillar on the porch rotted through. For a moment I could only sit and stare.

I shook off the lethargy, climbed out. From habit, I locked the door, then laughed at myself for bothering.

I stood for a moment breathing in the air. I saw that the barn had fallen; brush and tall weeds grew in the fields in back. Then like the boy I remembered, I started to walk up through the fields, beside the bank of the stream. Along the way I thought of that other walk, became for a time that long-ago boy.

The day was fresh then, the ground newly washed in a gentle rain. High grass, bent in the recent shower, curved back to dry in the sun. The boy trailed in his father's tracks; I trailed in my father's tracks. My father—the strongest man in the world. Omnipotent.

My cousin Donald was with us. Nearly my father's age, son of an elder sister, he'd completed basic training and was home on furlough. This walk was Donald's farewell to a place he loved, or so I later came to understand. I was too young then to realize all the implications of that long goodbye.

My father, whom someone later likened in build to a Greco-Roman wrestler, was talking about jujitsu. I'd seen the booklets he had, paper bound, filled with diagrams of men throwing and kicking each other.

I remembered sitting at the kitchen table, oil-cloth covered, the bare light bulb casting shadows through the room, my father turning the pages of these manuals.

"Roy," he told me, "learn to do these things, and you'll be at the mercy of no other human being."

I gazed fascinated at men being flipped over shoulders, twirled in somersaults, lifted by kicks. I'd rather run through my woods or wade the stream or race along the crest of a hill—alone. I had no quarrels with others, I thought. Or did I think that way? It hardly seems logical in light of my later needs.

Dad told my cousin Donald that he wasn't afraid of anyone. I accepted what he said, as is the nature of sons who haven't yet learned to rebel, who accept that their father can evoke the miraculous.

I loved my father. I thought him the equal at least of King Arthur or Gene Autry who rode across the screen at the movie theatre each Friday evening.

Suddenly, Donald came toward Dad, grabbed his arm and tossed him into the muddy bank of the stream. Stunned, Dad pushed himself to his knees, his gabardine slacks covered with dark brown mud, his glasses askew.

Imagine a child witnessing this scene. Imagine Donald standing and laughing. Imagine his saying, "That's what I think of your jujitsu." Imagine a father trying to rise, slipping in the mud, grabbing a tree limb, finally able to pull himself up, coming to stand again beside Donald.

I'd like to have smashed that grin from Donald's face. I'd like to have squashed him as one squashes a June bug accidentally underfoot. Instead, I swallowed hard and tried not to cry. I wanted the day to end; I wanted to be far away. I wanted to be back in Grandpa's kitchen with the kerosene lantern and dark wood cabinets.

In the same way men assess their lives, each of us reaches a milestone too when fathers become mere human beings. I hated my father then for being only a man. I hated Donald as much. I hoped he'd go to war and never come back. (In fact, he never did; I used to think he died in a place called Ju Jitsu. Later, I knew, of course, it was Iwo Jima.)

When we visited Grandpa after that, I stayed in the kitchen, or wandered in the other direction, out past the smokehouse, out to the deep mossy well.

I won a scholarship, earned my MBA, learned that I could be powerful too.

Now at that spot, or what I judged to be that spot, where Dad had been thrown by Donald, I let the scene play through my mind. Donald, twenty-two or twenty-three; my father, three or four years older. Kids. Not much more than kids who puff out their chests like banty roosters to prove they are men.

And I thought: Donald, I forgive you. I really didn't want you to die. What you did was not a mean thing; it was a natural thing. Both you and Dad were young men out to claim the world.

I glanced at my watch, smiled to myself. I should be just in time to meet Annabelle. We'd stay in the area a few more days, seeing the sights. Then we'd fly on home. Once there, I'd buy out that electronics firm. Why not? I could afford it.

THE END

Other Resources for Drama & Storytelling

STORYTELLING STEP-BY-STEP
by Marsh Cassady
Paperbound, $9.95, 156 pages, 5 ½" x 8 ½"
ISBN 0-89390-183-0

This is the basic handbook for storytellers. Marsh Cassady carefully breaks down the elements needed for successful storytelling. Find out about the relationship between the story and the teller. Learn how to adapt a story for a particular audience and how to hold that audience's attention; how to choose a story that matches the occasion; and how to use voice, gesture and props to enhance your storytelling. Plus, you can put theory into practice right in this book. Using his own stories for examples, the author asks you to change the point of view, find the theme, or adapt the stories as if you were going to tell them to your own audience. By the time you finish the book, you will have stories ready to tell!

ACTING STEP-BY-STEP
by Marsh Cassady
Paperbound, $9.95, 186 pages, 5 ½" x 8 ½"
ISBN 0-89390-120-2

Acting Step-by-Step challenges you to find and trust your creative abilities. It teaches you how to apply your creativity to situations where knowledge of acting is essential. For every field of work from politics to policy, from management to ministry, and, of course, for acting, this book will give you new insights on improving your presentation/performance. There are chapters on body language, voice, technique, character analysis, and more. Each chapter contains exercises to help you release creative energy, use imagination, and work to perfect art.

PLAYWRITING STEP-BY-STEP
by Marsh Cassady
Paperbound, $9.95, 113 pages, 5 ½" x 8 ½"
ISBN 0-89390-056-7

Describing writing as "ten percent inspiration and ninety percent perspiration," Marsh Cassady sets down the steps that make the ninety percent of writing a good play easier. With chapters devoted to plot, character, dialog, genre, writing, and marketing the play, this book is a comprehensive guide for the writer who is bursting with ideas, but hasn't got a clue how to develop them. Marsh Cassady—teacher, producer, writer, and editor—does know how to develop ideas, and he shares that skill with his readers.

For Using Stories in Ministry

STORY AS A WAY TO GOD
A Guide for Storytellers
by H. Maxwell Butcher
Paperbound, $11.95, 153 pages, 5 ½" x 8 ½"
ISBN 0-89390-201-2
This book will open your eyes to find God's story everywhere. The message of God is hidden in our novels, movies, poems, and plays. The homilist, the teacher, and the counselor will learn how to improve their storytelling skills as they read Maxwell Butcher's careful analysis of story type, from comedy and tragedy to melodrama and "resurrection literature." Tips include how to avoid a "too easy" ending, and why a story must "stretch" the reader. From *Sound of Music* to *Lord of the Rings*, the author convinces you that telling a story is the best way to share the Christian message, and he challenges you to be open to ways that you, too, can tell God's story.

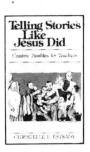

TELLING STORIES LIKE JESUS DID
Creative Parables for Teachers
by Christelle L. Estrada
Paperbound, $8.95, 100 pages, 5 ½" x 8 ½"
ISBN 0-89390-177-6
Christelle Estrada retells ten parables from Luke's Gospel; and after each parable, she reinterprets its message in terms today's children can understand. Teachers who are searching for a way to interpret the Gospel message of salvation for young people will find this book an excellent guide. Each chapter begins with one of the parables. Afterward, there is a period of reflection and questions to ask during that time. There are different questions for primary, intermediate, and junior-high levels. The author says that the word "salvation" originally meant "health and wholeness," and choosing to follow it is a move toward wholeness for a broken world. These stories will give you insight on how to interpret other Gospel stories, and they will make you pause and think about how you apply the Gospel in your own life.

Order from your bookseller, or use the form on the back of this page.

DIRECTING PUPPET THEATRE STEP-BY-STEP

by Carol Fijan and Frank Ballard with Christina Starobin
Paperbound, $14.95, 96 pages, 7" x 10"
ISBN 0-89390-126-1

Three gifted, award-winning puppeteers offer their expertise to the reader who wants to learn the rules of puppet theatre. From tips on how to design costumes and sets to the basic rules of all theatre, this book gives the reader information and inspiration. There are "how-to" diagrams, pictures of actual scenes and puppets, and "trade secrets" offered to help the reader develop or hone the skills of a good puppeteer. Whether you plan a career in puppet theatre or you want to use puppets in your classroom, religious education group, or Sunday school, this book will give you all the help you need.

PLAYS TO PLAY WITH IN CLASS

by Sally-Anne Milgrim
Paperbound, $10.95, 208 pages, 5 ½" x 8 ½"
ISBN 0-89390-060-5

Eight one-act plays for use in class dramatize the conflicts adolescents face as they struggle to grow and mature. The author, a noted professor of English and drama at Hunter College in New York City, suggests different ways the plays can be used. Each play is followed by series of questions: "How good is your understanding?" "You be the judge." "Try your hand as playwright." "This is your life." Some of the plays include songs, and the author invites her readers to compose songs for some of the other plays. This is a book for teachers, youth ministers, and school counselors. It offers a wealth of wonderful ways to draw adolescents out of themselves.

ORDER FORM

Order from your bookseller, or mail this form to:

QTY	TITLE	PRICE	TOTAL

Subtotal:_____
CA residents add 7¼% sales tax:_____
(Santa Clara Co. add 8¼% sales tax)
*Postage and handling:_____
Total amount:_____

*Postage and handling:
$2.00 for orders up to $20.00
10% of orders over $20.00 but less than $150.00
$15.00 for orders of $150.00 or more

RESOURCE Resource Publications, Inc.
160 E. Virginia St., Suite 290
San Jose, CA 95112-5876
or call (408) 286-8505
or fax (408) 287-8748

☐ My check or money order is enclosed.
☐ Charge my ☐ VISA ☐ MC Exp. date:_____

Card#_____-_____-_____-_____

Signature:_____

Name: _____

Institution:_____

Street: _____

City/St/Zip:_____